BMA's

TALENT & OLYMPIAD

EXAMS RESOURCE BOOK

CLASS V

Mathematics

BRAIN MAPPING
A C A D E M Y
Mapping Your Future

www.bmatalent.com

Published by:

Brain Mapping Academy

#16–11–16/1/B, First Floor, Farhath Hospital Road,
Saleem Nagar, Malakpet, Hyderabad–500 036.
© 040–66135169, 65165169.
E–mail: info@bmatalent.com
Website: www.bmatalent.com

ISBN : **978-93-82058-49-6**

Disclaimer

Every care has been taken by the compilers and
publishers to give correct, complete and updated information.
In case there is any omission, printing mistake or any
other error which might have crept in inadvertently,
neither the compiler / publisher nor any of the
distributors take any legal responsibility.

*In case of any dispute, all matters are subjected to the exclusive
jurisdiction of the courts in Hyderabad only.*

First Edition   : 2003

Second Edition   : 2008

Revised Edition : 2015

Printed at:
Sri Vinayaka Art Printers, Hyderabad.

Publisher's Note

Sometimes the understanding of fundamental concepts alone does not help the students to crack the competitive exams as most of them are objective in structure. Students need rigorous training to familiarize themselves to the style of the exams they are attempting. The board exams which are of qualifying, but not competitive, nature do not completely address the needs of students in testing them in objective type format.

To bridge this gap and to enable the students to face the reality of competitive exams, Brain Mapping Academy, brought out an all-objective questions reference book.

A crisp summary of the topics and useful equations were provided at the beginning of each chapter so that the students can memorize the important points.

Care has been taken to design thought-provoking questions. These should help students to attain a deeper understanding of principles. The questions have been reviewed to fill the gaps in problem coverage and to build the confidence in the students. They have also been expanded to impart reasoning/logical/analytical skills.

This book will cater all the requirements of the students who are approaching national/state level talent search examinations and all Olympiad exams. This book also complements the additional preparation needs of the students for the regular board exams.

We took utmost care to make this the best resource book available for the talent / olympiad exams aspirants. We welcome criticism from the students, teacher community and educators, especially concerning any errors and deficiencies which may have remained in this edition and the suggestions for improvement for the next edition.

NATIONAL LEVEL SCIENCE TALENT SEARCH EXAMINATION

Aim of this examination

The focus on fundamentals is so important that without a firm understanding of them, a child cannot be expected to face the reality of the competitive world once he/she finishes the formal education. Even while opting for higher studies the student has to go through a complete scan of what he/she knows. Exams like IIT-JEE, AIEEE, AIIMS, AFMC, CAT, SAT, GRE, GMAT, etc. are so designed to test the fundamental strength of a student. Hence the need of the hour is building the fundamental base as strong as possible.

A successful life emerges out from healthy and sound competition. Competition is the only way for the students to shake lethargy. It's the only way to get introduced for manly worthiness. Firm standards in education and competition are the tonic for a promising and talented future.

This exactly is the philosophy behind the Unified Council's NSTSE.

Organisation

National Science Talent Search Examination is conducted by Unified Council. Unified Council is India's first ISO 9001 certified organisation in the educational testing and assessment. Since its inception, Unified Council has put together the best brains in an endeavour to make the younger generation fundamentally stronger and nourish their brains for a bright and enterprising future.

Eligibility : Students of classes 1, 2, 3, 4, 5, 6, 7, 8, 9, 10, 11 & 12 are eligible to participate in this examination.

Medium & Syllabus: This exam is conducted in only English medium and is suitable for all the students following CBSE/ICSE/State Board Syllabi.

Examination Pattern

There will be a separate question paper for each class. All questions are objective-type multiple choice with no negative marking for wrong answers.

Duration: 90 minutes

Date : Conducted every year on the last Sunday of January.

Test Centres : Spread across the country.

DIVISION OF MARKS

FOR CLASS I		
Mathematics	:	25 marks
General Science	:	15 Marks
FOR CLASS II		
Mathematics	:	25 marks
General Science	:	25 Marks
FOR CLASS III		
Mathematics	:	40 marks
General Science	:	35 Marks
FOR CLASSES IV & V		
Mathematics	:	45 marks
General Science	:	45 Marks
General Questions	:	10 marks

FOR CLASSES VI TO X		
Mathematics	:	25 marks
Physics	:	25 marks
Chemistry	:	20 marks
Biology	:	20 marks
General Questions	:	10 marks
FOR CLASS XI & XII(PCM)		
Mathematics	:	40 marks
Physics	:	25 marks
Chemistry	:	25 marks
General Questions	:	10 marks
FOR CLASS XI & XII(PCB)		
Biology	:	40 marks
Physics	:	25 marks
Chemistry	:	25 marks
General Questions	:	10 marks

Infrastructure

The Council makes use of ultra-modern equipment such as *Optical Mark Recognition (OMR)* equipment to evaluate the answer papers to proficiently assess students' performance. The examination procedure is **completely computerised.**

Unique Service from Unified Council:

Unique analysis reports like Student's Performance Report for students, General School Report & Individual School Report for schools provided. These reports are very much helpful for students & schools to analyse their strengths and weaknesses.

General School Report (GSR) analyses the performance of students participating in the exam (subject-wise and class-wise). The report, in graphical format will have Ogive and Histogram Graphs, which are useful to schools that wish to improve their students' performance by benchmarking the areas of weaknesses and building upon them.

Individual School Report (ISR) analyses the performance of a particular school when compared to the rest of the students participating in this examination (subject-wise, class-wise and question-wise). This report acts as a tool for the schools to improve their students' performance in the future by benchmarking the areas of weaknesses and building upon them.

Awards & Scholarships:

Top 100 members in each class will be awarded with Awards & Medals etc.

UNIFIED COUNCIL
An ISO 9001: 2008 Certified Organisation
Foundation for success

#16-11-16/1/B, Farhath Hospital Road, Saleem Nagar, Malakpet, Hyderabad-500 036
Phones : 040-24557708, 24545862, 66139917
E-mail: exam@unifiedcouncil.com, Website: www.unifiedcouncil.com

CONTENTS

Mathematics

Large Numbers

♦ **Indian place value chart for a 9-digit number:**

Period	Crores		Lakhs		Thousands		Ones		
Place	T.C	C	T.L	L	T.Th	Th	H	T	O

♦ **International place value chart for a 9 digit number:**

Period	Millions			Thousands			Ones		
Place	H.M	T.M	M	H.Th	T.Th	Th	H	T	O

> 1 million = 10 lakhs
> 10 million = 1 crore
> 100 million = 10 crores

♦ **Inserting commas:**

A comma is inserted after each period in both the systems of numeration.

1 lakh = 1,00,000

1 million = 1,000,000

♦ **Place value of a digit:**

e.g., In 7308, 7 is in the thousands place.

So, its place value is 7000.

♦ **Face value of a digit:**

Face value of a digit is the value of the digit itself.

In 7308, face value of 7 is 7.

In 390876, 9 is in ten thousands place.

So, its place value is 90000.

Its face value is 9.

♦ **Expanded form of a number:**

A number written as the sum of the place values of its digits is said to be in its expanded form.

e.g., 90,63,52,146

= 900000000 + 0 + 6000000 + 300000 + 50000 + 2000 + 100 + 40 + 6

♦ **Comparing numbers:**

(a) Count the number of digits of the numbers to be compared. The number with more number of digits is greater and that with less number of digits is smaller.

e.g., 10612 > 621

(b) If the number of digits is equal, compare the values of the digits from left to right in both the numbers.

e.g., 4261 > 4216

♦ **Fundamental operations:**

The four basic mathematical operations are addition (+), subtraction (−), multiplication (×) and division (÷).

♦ **Addition:**

The numbers that are added are called **addends**. The number obtained on adding two numbers is called **sum**.

When any number is added to '0', the sum is the number itself.

e.g., $0 + 6 = 6$

The sum of two numbers is always greater than each of the addends (provided none of the addends is "0".)

♦ **Subtraction:**

The greater number in subtraction is called **minuend**. The smaller number being subtracted is called **subtrahend**. The number obtained on subtraction is called **difference**.

When '0' is subtracted from a number, the difference is the number itself.

e.g., $15 - 0 = 15$

♦ **Multiplication:**

Factor × Factor = Product

Multiplicand × Multiplier = Product

When any number is multiplied by 1, the product is the number itself.

e.g., $92 \times 1 = 92$

When any number is multiplied by 0, the product is zero.

e.g., $61 \times 0 = 0$

♦ **Division:**

e.g., 6) 12 (2
　　　 −12
　　　 ――――
　　　　 0
　　　 ――――

6 is divisor; 12 is dividend; 2 is quotient; and 0 is remainder.

1. Large Numbers

♦ **Verification:**

Dividend = Divisor × Quotient + Remainder

'0' divided by any number is '0'.

e.g., 0 ÷ 5 = 0

Division by 0 is not defined.

Any number divided by '1' is the number itself.

e.g., 19 ÷ 1 = 19

♦ **Divisibility Tests:**

Test by 2:

A number is divisible by 2 if it has 0, 2, 4, 6 or 8 in its ones place.

e.g., 7034<u>2</u>

The digit in the ones place of 70342 is 2.

∴ 70342 is divisible by 2.

Test by 3:

A number is divisible by 3 if the sum of the digits in the number is divisible by 3.

e.g., 654

6 + 5 + 4 = 15 is divisible by 3.

So, 654 is divisible by 3.

Test by 4:

A number is divisible by 4 if the number formed by the digits in its ones and tens places is divisible by 4.

e.g., 67<u>32</u>

Since 32 is divisible by 4, 6732 is divisible by 4.

Test by 5:

A number is divisible by 5 if it has 0 or 5 in its ones place.

e.g., 710<u>0</u> ; 3162<u>5</u> etc, are divisible by 5.

Test by 6:

A number is divisible by 6 if it is divisible by both 2 and 3.

e.g., 171312

In 171312, the digit in ones place is 2. So, 171312 is divisible by 2.

1 + 7 + 1 + 3 + 1 + 2 = 15 is divisible by 3.

So, 171312 is divisible by 3.

Hence, 171312 is divisible by 6.

Test by 8:

A number is divisible by 8 if the number formed by the digits in its ones, tens and hundreds places is divisible by 8.

e.g., 74<u>168</u>

168 is divisible by 8. So, 74168 is divisible by 8.

Test by 9:

A number is divisible by 9 if the sum of its digits is divisible by 9.

e.g., 345285

$3 + 4 + 5 + 2 + 8 + 5 = 27$ is divisible by 9.

So, 345285 is divisible by 9.

Test by 10:

A number is divisible by 10 if the digit in the ones place is 0.

e.g., 8431<u>0</u>

The ones digit in 84310 is 0. So, it is divisible by 10.

Test by 11:

A number is divisible by 11 if the difference of sums of digits in the even and odd places is 0 or a multiple of 11.

e.g., 75354312

$5 + 5 + 3 + 2 = 15$

$7 + 3 + 4 + 1 = 15$

$15 - 15 = 0$

So, the number is divisible by 11.

◆ **Rounding numbers:**

(a) **To the nearest ten:**

Step 1: If the digit in the ones place is 0, 1, 2, 3 or 4, replace it by zero.

Step 2: If the digit in the ones palce is 5, 6, 7, 8 or 9, replace it by zero and increase the digit in the tens place by 1.

(b) **To the nearest hundred:**

Step 1: If the digit in the tens place is 0, 1, 2, 3 or 4, replace the digits in tens and ones place by zeroes.

Step 2: If the digit in the tens place is 5, 6, 7, 8 or 9, replace the digits in tens and ones places by zeroes and increase the digit in the hundreds place by 1.

(c) **To the nearest thousand:**

Step 1: If the digit in the hundreds place is 0, 1, 2, 3 or 4, replace the digits in the hundreds, tens and ones places by zeroes.

Step 2: If the digit in the hundreds place is 5, 6, 7, 8 or 9, replace the digits in the hundreds, tens and ones places by zeroes and increase the digit in the thousands place by 1.

Place to which a number is to be estimated	Place of the digit to be considered	Value of the digit considered	What must be done?	Examples
10	Ones	0 – 4	Replace ones digit with 0.	144; 4 < 5 ; So, 144 rounded to the nearest 10 is 140.
		5 – 9	Replace ones digit with 0. Add 1 to tens digit.	177; 7 > 5 ; So, 177 rounded to the nearest 10 is 180.
100	Tens	0 – 4	Replace ones and tens digits with 0.	1137; 3 < 5 ; So, 1137 rounded to the nearest 100 is 1100.
		5 – 9	Replace ones digit with 0. Add 1 to hundreds digit.	1268 ; 6 > 5 ; So, 1268 rounded to the nearest 100 is 1300.
1000	Hundreds	0 – 4	Replace ones, tens and hundreds digits with 0.	5472 ; 4 < 5 ; So, 5472 rounded to the nearest 1000 is 5000.
		5 – 9	Replace ones, tens and hundreds digits with 0. Add 1 to thousands digit.	2734 ; 7 > 5 ; So, 2734 rounded to the nearest 1000 is 3000.

◆ **Roman Numerals:**

The digits 0, 1, 2, ..., 9 were first used by the Hindus and then the Arabs. So, these digits are called Hindu-Arabic numerals.

Romans used the Roman Numeration system.

It has 7 symbols called Roman Numerals.

Roman Numerals	I	V	X	L	C	D	M
Hindu-Arabic Numerals	1	5	10	50	100	500	1000

> *Note:* There is no symbol for zero and no place value in the Roman system.

◆ **Rules for writing Roman Numerals:**

(a) If a smaller numeral is written after a larger numeral, their values are added.

e.g., (i) VIII = 5 + 1 + 1 = 8

(ii) LX = 50 + 10 = 60

(b) If a smaller numeral is written before a larger numeral, its value is subtracted from that of the larger numeral.

1. Large Numbers   13

e.g., (i) IX = 10 – 1 = 9

(ii) XL = 50 – 10 = 40

(c) Repetition of a numeral means addition.

> **Note:** A Roman numeral can be repeated to a maximum of three times.

e.g., (i) XXX = 10 + 10 + 10 = 30

(ii) CCC = 100 + 100 + 100 = 300

(d) If a smaller numeral is placed between two larger numerals, the value of the smaller numeral is subtracted from the value of the larger numeral following it.

e.g., (i) XIX = 10 + (10 – 1) = 10 + 9 = 19 (and not 10 + 1 + 10 = 21)

(ii) CXL = 100 + (50 – 10) = 100 + 40 = 140 (and not 100 + 10 + 50 = 160)

- **Remember :** (a) V is never repeated.

  (b) V can never be subtracted from X.

  (c) I can be subtracted only from V and X.

- **Numerical Expression:**

Expressions written using numerals and symbols are called numerical expressions.

BODMAS: The rule for evaluating expressions is BODMAS rule, which gives the order in which an expression is to be evaluated. If BODMAS rule is not used, different answers are obtained by different persons.

We use DMAS rule to simplify the numerical expressions.

D – Division   M – Multiplication

A – Addition   S – Subtraction

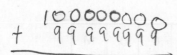

$$+\ \begin{array}{r} 100000000 \\ 99999999 \\ \hline \end{array}$$

$$\begin{array}{r} 9999999 \\ -\ 10000 \\ \hline 9989999 \end{array}$$

Multiple Choice Questions

1 With which place does a 7-digit number start in the Indian system?

(A) Lakhs   (B) Ten thousands
(C) Ten lakhs   (D) Crores

2 Identify the place with which an 8-digit number starts in the International system.

(A) Millions
(B) Ten millions
(C) Hundred thousands
(D) Lakhs

3 Find the place value of 0 in 36,04,85,298.

(A) Ten lakhs   (B) Lakhs
(C) Zero   (D) 6 crores

4 Find the sum of the greatest 8-digit number and the smallest 9-digit number.

(A) 1,99,99,999   (B) 19,99,99,999
(C) 99,99,99,999 (D) 1,00,00,999

5 What is the difference of the greatest 7-digit number and the smallest 5 digit number?

(A) 9,98,999   (B) 99,89,999
(C) 99,899   (D) 9,98,099

6 By how many times do the place values of the digits increase from right to left in a number?

(A) 100   (B) $\dfrac{1}{10}$
(C) 10   (D) 1000

7 How many crores is 10 million?

(A) 10   (B) 1
(C) 5   (D) 100

8 How many zeroes follow 1 in the numeral for 10 millions?

(A) 8   (B) 7
(C) 6   (D) 9

9 Identify the number name for 123,080,603.

(A) One two three eighty thousand six hundred three.

(B) One hundred twenty three million eight thousand six hundred three.

(C) One hundred twenty three million eighty thousand six hundred three.

(D) One twenty three million eighty thousand six hundred.

10 Identify the equivalent of 10 crores from the following.

(A) 10 millions   (B) 100 millions
(C) 1 million   (D) 1000 millions

11 Observe the following.

$$6, 73, 89, 145 \boxed{<} 67, 38, 91, 450$$

Identify the missing symbol.

(A) <   (B) >
(C) =   (D) Either (B) or (C)

12 What is the missing digit in 3 ☐ 6013 if 3 ☐ 6013 = 300000 + 70000 + 6000 + 0 + 10 + 3?

(A) 3   (B) 6
(C) 1   (D) 7

13 In 189485, how many times the value of 8 in the tens place is the value of 8 in the ten thousands place?

(A) 10   (B) 1000
(C) 100   (D) 10000

14 Which of the following is the best estimate of the product 5842 × 49?

(A) 250000   (B) 292000
(C) 290000   (D) 300000

15 Identify the smallest 7-digit number.

(A) 10,00,000

(B) 1 + greatest 6 digit number

(C) Both (A) and (B)

(D) Neither (A) nor (B)

16 What is the difference between the place value and face value of 5 in 91,25,678?

(A) 4995   (B) 0

(C) 4095   (D) 5000

17 Study the following equation.

$$792 \times 650 = 800 \times 650 - \square \times \square$$

What is the value of the product of the missing numbers?

(A) 520   (B) 5020

(C) 5200   (D) 8650

18 What is the difference between the smallest 6-digit odd number and the largest 4-digit even number?

(A) 90002   (B) 90003

(C) 101113   (D) 101121

19 For which digit is the place value and face value always the same?

(A) 0   (B) 10

(C) Any digit   (D) 100

20 Find the numeral for sixty million and sixty six.

(A) 60,000,060   (B) 60,000,066

(C) 6,000,066   (D) 600,000,060

21 Which of the following numbers has the greatest value for digit 5?

(A) 80503   (B) 5098

(C) 146857   (D) 7653231

22 The digits 6,0,3,7,6 and 9 are arranged to form the greatest possible 6-digit odd number. Find the difference in value of the two digits 6.

(A) 5400   (B) 540

(C) 54600   (D) 54000

23 Which of the following is equal to 75×100?

(A) $75 \times 20 \times 5$

(B) $70 + 5 \times 100$

(C) $75 \times 10 + 90$

(D) $(75 \times 20) + (75 \times 5)$

24 The odometer of a car shows 9232 km. How many thousand kilometres is the reading?

(A) 10   (B) 8

(C) 11   (D) 9

25 Find the value of 100 ten thousands 65 thousands 50 hundreds 2 ones?

(A) 10,07,002   (B) 10,70,002

(C) 10,65,502   (D) 1,00,70,002

26 For how many hundreds does the digit 9 stand in the product of 255 and 37?

(A) 9000   (B) 90

(C) 90000   (D) 9

27 What is the largest possible whole number which results in 223000 when a number is rounded off to the nearest thousand?

(A) 223499   (B) 223001

(C) 223500   (D) 223100

28 Observe the number line given.

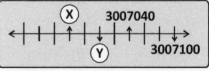

What is the difference of X and Y?

(A) 4060   (B) 400

(C) 4040   (D) 40

29 How many hundreds must be added to 30 thousands to get 1 million?

(A) 97   (B) 9700

(C) 97000   (D) 970000

30 What is the sum of the values of the digit '8' in 438498?

(A) 16   (B) 88
(C) 808   (D) 8008

31 M is the largest number which when rounded off to the nearest hundreds gives 63500. N is the smallest number which when rounded off to the nearest thousands gives 150000. What is the sum of M and N?

(A) 202049   (B) 231409
(C) 213049   (D) 213490

32 Find the number which is divisible by 2.

(A) 7907   (B) 63195
(C) 72028   (D) 3451

33 By which two numbers must a number be divisible so that it is divisible by 6?

(A) 4 and 3   (B) 2 and 4
(C) 2 and 3   (D) 3 and 5

34 What is the smallest possible 5-digit even number that can be formed using all the digits in the sum of 82349 and 8268?

(A) 10769   (B) 16790
(C) 10796   (D) 19706

35 Which of the following is the number obtained by rounding 178762 to the nearest hundreds?

(A) 178760   (B) 178800
(C) 178700   (D) 17800

36 Identify the number obtained by rounding 38,65,62,048 to the nearest lakhs.

(A) 386860000   (B) 3865600
(C) 386500000   (D) 386600000

37 The difference of two numbers is 174325. If the greater number is 8765432, what is the smaller number?

(A) 8590107   (B) 8591107
(C) 8592107   (D) 8519107

38 In a school, there are a total of 2476 students and teachers. The total number of teachers and boys is 1289. The total number of girls and teachers is 1246. How many teachers are there in the school?

(A) 80   (B) 70
(C) 65   (D) 59

 Previous Contest Questions

1 Some Roman numerals are given in the box.

I C L M D

Which of the following is the number that can be written using all the given Roman numerals?

(A) 1775   (B) 864
(C) 1947   (D) 1753

2 Study the Hindu-Arabic equivalents of the given Roman numbers.

(i)   DCLV = 655
(ii)   XLVI = 46
(iii) MDCL = 1560

Which of the following is/are correct?

(A) Only (i) and (ii)
(B) Only (ii) and (iii)
(C) Only (i) and (iii)
(D) Only (i)

3 ·Observe the given figure.

Who has the largest number?

(A) R   (B) Q
(C) P   (D) S

4 How many match sticks are needed to make the Roman numerals equivalent to 29?

(A) 6   (B) 7
(C) 9   (D) 10

5 Find the Roman numeral for 1618.

(A) MDCXVIII   (B) MDCLXVI
(C) MCDXVIII   (D) MDCLXVIII

6 Which of these numbers has the least value?

(A) CDCX   (B) CDXL
(C) DCLX   (D) DCXL

7 What is the order in which numerical expressions are to be evaluated?

(A) M, A, S, D   (B) D, S, M, A
(C) D, A, S, M   (D) D, M, A S

8 What is the resultant of the given expression?

$$30 \times 8 \div 2 + 62 - 24$$

(A) 168   (B) 158
(C) 185   (D) 142

9 Identify the missing term in the equation.

$$909000 \div 9090 = 159 - \boxed{?}$$

(A) 159   (B) 100
(C) 59   (D) 95

10 How is the expression $100 - 7 \times 1 + 5$ written using brackets?

(A) $(100 - 7) \times (1 + 5)$
(B) $(100 - 7) \times 1 + 5$
(C) $100 - 7 \times (1 + 5)$
(D) $100 - (7 \times 1) + 5$

◇ ◇ ◇

Synopsis

♦ **Factors:** The numbers that are multiplied to give a product are called factors.

e.g., $43 \times 15 = 645$

    Factor Factor Product

Factors divide the number exactly (i.e., without leaving a remainder.) So, factors are also called divisors.

1 is a factor of every number, and every number is a factor of itself.

1 is the smallest factor of a number and the number itself is its greatest factor.

The factor of a number is less than or equal to the number.

Every number (except 1) has at least 2 factors – 1 and the number itself.

The factors or divisors that are common to two or more numbers are called their common factors.

e.g., Factors of 4 are ①, ②, 4. Factors of 6 are ①, ②, 3, 6.

    ∴ Common factors of 4 and 6 are 1, 2.

♦ **Highest Common Factor (H.C.F):** The highest of the common factors of two or more numbers is called their Highest Common Factor (H.C.F.) or their Greatest Common Divisor (G.C.D.).

♦ **Multiples:** The products obtained when a number is multiplied by 1, 2, 3, 4 and so on are called the multiples of that number.

e.g., 4, 8, 12, 16, 20, ... are the multiples of 4.

    8, 16, 24, 32, 40, ... are the multiples of 8.

Every number is a multiple of 1.

A number is the smallest multiple of itself.

Every multiple of a number is greater than or equal to the number itself.

Multiples of a number are infinite. There is no largest multiple of a number.

The multiples that are common to two or more numbers are called their common multiples.

e.g.,   Multiples of 2 are 2, 4, ⑥, 8, 10, ⑫, 14, 16, ⑱, ...

Multiples of 6 are ⑥, ⑫, ⑱, 24, 30, 36, 42, ...

∴ Common multiples of 2 and 6 are 6, 12, 18, ...

◆ **Least Common Multiple (L.C.M.):** The lowest of the common multiples of two or more numbers is called their Lowest (or Least) Common Multiple (L.C.M.).

◆ **Even numbers:** The numbers which are multiples of 2 are called even numbers.

e.g., 438, 1450, 7034 etc.,

◆ **Odd numbers:** The numbers other than the multiples of 2 are called odd numbers.

e.g., 215, 6013, 897 etc.,

◆ **Prime numbers:** The numbers which have only 1 and itself as factors are called prime numbers.

e.g., 3, 11, 23, 47, etc.,

◆ **Composite numbers:** The numbers which have at least 1 factor other than 1 and itself are called composite numbers.

e.g., 4, 9, 76, 108 etc.,

a) 1 is neither prime nor composite.

b) 2 is the smallest and the only even prime number.

c) 4 is the smallest composite number.

d) Prime numbers other than 2 are odd.

◆ **Twin primes:** Two consecutive prime numbers that differ by 2 are called twin primes.

e.g., (3, 5), (5, 7), (11, 13) etc.,

◆ **Co-prime numbers:** The numbers which have no common factor except 1 are called co-prime numbers.

e.g., (4, 15), (11, 17), (18, 37) etc.,

◆ **Prime factorisation:** The process of splitting a given number into its prime factors is called prime factorisation.

◆ **Methods to find the H.C.F. of the given numbers:**

a) **Listing the factors:**

e.g., Find the H.C.F. of 36 and 72.

Step 1: List all the factors of the given numbers.

Factors of 36: 1, 2, 3, 4, 6, 9, 12, 18, 36

Factors of 72: 1, 2, 3, 4, 6, 8, 9, 12, 18, 24, 36, 72

Step 2: Find the common factors of the given numbers.

The common factors of 36 and 72 are 1, 2, 3, 4, 6, 9, 12, 18 and 36.

Step 3: The greatest of the common factors is the required H.C.F.

36 is the greatest of the common factors of 36 and 72.

∴ 36 is the required H. C. F.

b) Prime factorisation:

e.g., Find the H. C. F. of 36 and 72.

Step 1: Express the given numbers as the product of prime numbers.

$36 = 2 \times 2 \times 3 \times 3$

$72 = 2 \times 2 \times 2 \times 3 \times 3$

Step 2: Circle their common prime factors.

$36 = ②\times②\times③\times③$

$72 = ②\times②\times2\times③\times③$

Step 3: Consider one set of the common factors and find their product.

$2 \times 2 \times 3 \times 3 = 36$

Step 4: The product obtained in step 3 is the required H. C. F.

Hence, the H. C. F. of 36 and 72 is 36.

c) Division method:

e.g., Find the H.C.F of 36, 72 and 144.

Step 1: Divide the larger number by the smallest number.

```
36)72(2
   -72
   ___
    0
```

Step 2: If the remainder is not zero, divide the divisor by the remainder. Continue the procedure until the remainder obtained is 0.

If the remainder obtained is 0, divide the other given number by the divisor.

```
36)144(2
   -144
   ____
     0
```

Step 3:   If the remainder is 0, the divisor is the Highest Common Factor or Greatest Common Divisor of the given numbers.

Thus, 36 is the H. C. F. (or G. C. D.) of 36, 72 and 144.

◆ **Methods to find the L.C.M. of the given numbers:**

a) Listing the multiples:

e.g., Find the L.C.M. of 36 and 72.

Step 1:   **List the first few multiples of the given numbers.**

Multiples of 36 : 36, 72, 108, 144, 180, 216, . . .

Multiples of 72 : 72, 144, 216, . . .

Step 2:   **Find the common multiples of the given numbers.**

The common multiples of 36 and 72 are 72, 144, 216, . . .

Step 3:   **The lowest of the common multiples is the required L.C.M.**

72 is the lowest of the common multiples of 36 and 72.

Hence, 72 is the required L.C.M.

b) Prime factorisation method:

e.g., Find the L.C.M. of 36 and 72.

Step 1:   **Express the given numbers as the product of prime numbers.**

$36 = 2 \times 2 \times 3 \times 3$

$72 = 2 \times 2 \times 2 \times 3 \times 3$

Step 2:   **Circle their common prime factors.**

$36 = ②×②×③×③$

$72 = ②×②×2×③×③$

Step 3:   **Consider one set of the common factors and find their product.**

$2 \times 2 \times 3 \times 3 = 36$

Step 4:   **Find the product of the remaining factors (uncircled factors) and the product obtained in step 3.**

$36 \times 2 = 72$

Step 5:   **The product obtained in step 4 is the required L.C.M.**

Hence, the L.C.M. of 36 and 72 is 72.

c) Division Method:

e.g., Find the L.C.M. of 36 and 72.

2. Factors and Multiples

Step 1:   Write the given numbers separated by commas between them.

$\underline{|36,\ 72}$

Step 2:   Divide the given numbers by a prime factor common to them.

$\underline{2\,|\,36,\ 72}$
$\quad\ 18,\ 36$

> *Note:* Start with the least prime factor common to the given numbers.

Step 3:   Continue the process until all the factors are prime.

$2\,\underline{|\,36,\ 72}$
$2\,\underline{|\,18,\ 36}$
$3\,\underline{|\ \ 9,\ 18}$
$3\,\underline{|\ \ 3,\ 6}$
$\quad\ \ 1,\ 2$

Step 4:   Find the product of all the prime factors obtained in step 3, which gives the required L.C.M.

$2 \times 2 \times 3 \times 3 \times 2 = 72$

Therefore, 72 is the L.C.M. of 36 and 72.

◆   L. C. M. of given numbers = Their H. C. F × The product of the prime factors left uncircled.

Multiple Choice Questions    A B C D

1 Which of the following are two consecutive prime numbers that differ by 2?

(A) Co-primes
(B) Twin primes
(C) Composite numbers
(D) Both (A) and (B)

2 Identify the numbers with only 1 as their common factor.

(A) Co-prime numbers
(B) Twin prime numbers
(C) Composite numbers
(D) Prime numbers

3 Find the smallest whole number that is divisible by 10 and 12.

(A) 40   (B) 30
(C) 72   (D) 60

4 Which of the following are not multiples of 2?

(A) Even numbers
(B) Odd numbers
(C) Prime numbers
(D) Composite numbers

5 Which type of numbers have more than two factors?

(A) Even numbers
(B) Prime numbers
(C) Composite numbers
(D) Odd numbers

6 Stamps in an album can be arranged as 12 per page or 18 per page exactly. What is the greatest number of stamps one can have if they are fewer than 500?

(A) 468   (B) 540
(C) 504   (D) 432

7 What is the L.C.M. of two co-prime numbers?

(A) Their sum   (B) Their difference
(C) Their product (D) Their quotient

8 Study the numbers given in the box.

5760		720
	1080	
2160		1440

Identify the number that is not a divisor of the given numbers.

(A) 23   (B) 24
(C) 36   (D) 12

9 Find the L.C.M. of 12, 24 and 36.

(A) 36   (B) 24
(C) 72   (D) 108

10 Identify an example for twin primes.

(A) 5, 11   (B) 3, 5
(C) 11, 17   (D) 3, 7

11 What is the H.C.F. of 36 and 144?

(A) 36   (B) 144
(C) 4   (D) 2

12 What is the H.C.F. of two co-prime numbers?

(A) 1   (B) 0
(C) 2   (D) Their product

13 P is the least common multiple of 45 and 50. What is the value of 10P + 100?

(A) 4500   (B) 4600
(C) 4400   (D) 1000

14 What are the common factors of 9 and 36?

(A) 1, 3, 9   (B) 1, 4, 3, 5, 9
(C) 1, 4, 5   (D) 1, 3, 4, 9

15 Find three common multiples of 18 and 6.

(A) 18, 6, 9   (B) 18, 36, 6
(C) 36, 54, 72   (D) 1, 6, 18

16 When a number is increased by 8, it is divisible by 35. What is the remainder when the same number is divided by 5?

(A) 2   (B) 4
(C) 3   (D) 0

17 The largest number less than 100 divisible by 15 is decreased by 5. Which of these is a factor of the resultant number?

(A) 23   (B) 17
(C) 25   (D) 19

18 How many prime numbers are there from 50 to 100?

(A) 18   (B) 12
(C) 10   (D) 20

19 How is 20 written as the product of primes?

(A) 2×5 (B) $2 \times 2 \times 3 \times 5$
(C) $2 \times 2 \times 5$ (D) $2 \times 2 \times 3$

20 Identify the correct statement.

(A) The L.C.M. of two co-primes is their product.

(B) The H.C.F. of twin primes is their product.

(C) The largest factor of a number is 1.

(D) The smallest factor of a number is the number itself.

21 Which of the following sets of numbers have the same H.C.F.?

60		120	135
650	230	180	315
250	450	240	495
P	Q	R	S

(A) Q and R   (B) P and R
(C) R and S   (D) P and Q

22 How many times the H.C.F. of 11, 33 and 88 is their L.C.M.?

(A) 11   (B) 24
(C) 22   (D) 3629

23 Identify an example for co-prime numbers.

(A) 25, 14   (B) 18, 16
(C) 9, 18   (D) 11, 77

24 The L.C.M. of two numbers is 10 times their H.C.F. Find the numbers.

(A) 24, 96   (B) 16, 15
(C) 24, 480   (D) 24, 240

25 What is the sum of the first five multiples of 8?

(A) 90   (B) 60
(C) 30   (D) 120

26 Find the least 4 - digit number that is divisible by 8.

(A) 1000   (B) 1008
(C) 4000   (D) 1016

27 Find the product of all the factors of 40.

(A) 265×100 (B) 256×10000
(C) 256×1000 (D) 265×1000

28 How many factors does 256 have?

(A) 9   (B) 8
(C) 10   (D) 12

29 How many hundreds are there in the sum of the factors of 140?

(A) 300   (B) 30
(C) 336   (D) 3

30 X is the sum of the factors of 84. Which of the following is a correct statement?

(A) The digits in hundreds and tens places of the sum are the same.

(B) The digit in ones place is the same as the digit in tens place.

(C) The digit in hundreds place is the same as the digit in ones place.

(D) The digit in ones place is the least.

2. Factors and Multiples

31 A and B are two 1 - digit numbers such that A × A × B × B = 2025. What are the respective values of A and B?

(A) 5, 9   (B) 5, 3
(C) 9, 4   (D) 2, 5

32 Observe the twin primes in the table.

(3, 5)	(5, 7)	(11,13)	(17,19)
P	Q	R	S

Which of the given twin primes are present in the prime factorisation of 2145?

(A) Q and R   (B) P and S
(C) P and Q   (D) P and R

33 Identify the number whose prime factorisation has three 2's, four 3's and a 5.

(A) 3240   (B) 2430
(C) 3420   (D) 2304

34 A box had some pens in it. When the pens are distributed equally to 18 children, none remained but while distributing to 19 children, 5 children got 1 pen less than the others. How many pens were there in the box?

(A) 70   (B) 76
(C) 90   (D) 85

35 Aakash's age is a factor of 14. Next year his age will be a multiple of 5. How old will he be in 6 years' time?

(A) 15 years   (B) 21 years
(C) 14 years   (D) 20 years

36 What is the sum of the numbers that are multiples of 7 as well as factors of 42?

(A) 84   (B) 42
(C) 14   (D) 7

37 Study the information given in the box.

★ X is a multiple of 6.
★ X is a factor of 84.

What is the value of X?

(A) 42   (B) 26
(C) 21   (D) 14

38 P is a 2 - digit common factor of 36 and 24. Q is a number that is both a factor and multiple of 28. What is the value of P + Q?

(A) 24   (B) 28
(C) 12   (D) 40

39 When a number X is added to 8, the sum is divisible by 14. What could the number X be?

(A) 48   (B) 58
(C) 78   (D) 68

40 The quotient when a number is divided by 5 is 6. What is the quotient when the same number is divided by 30?

(A) 1   (B) 100
(C) 10   (D) 1000

41 How many twin primes are there between 1 and 100?

(A) 6   (B) 10
(C) 7   (D) 8

42 Which of these numbers has 2, 3, 4 and 10 as factors?

(A) 20709   (B) 108240
(C) 18045   (D) 20801

43 Study the following.

★ M is the least common multiple of 18, 24 and 40.
★ N is the highest common factor of 60, 180 and 360.

Which digit in the number 2M + 15N is in the thousands place?

(A) 0   (B) 1
(C) 2   (D) 6

Previous Contest Questions

1 Two toy trains start at the same time. The first one stops after every 5 seconds and the second one stops after every 4 seconds. How many times do they stop together in 1 minute?

(A) 4   (B) 2
(C) 3   (D) 5

2 17, 19, p, 29, 31, q, 41 is a list of prime numbers in ascending order. What is the value of q – p?

(A) 60   (B) 37
(C) 23   (D) 14

3 Which of the following numbers has 8 as factor?

(A) 136   (B) 228
(C) 842   (D) 748

4 The L.C.M. of 3, 6 and x is 18. What is the possible value of x?

(A) 36   (B) 6
(C) 18   (D) 3

5 Given that (p + 3) is the highest common factor of 81 and 108, find the value of p.

(A) 6   (B) 12
(C) 9   (D) 24

6 m is a multiple of 8 and a factor of 48. Find the possible value for m.

(A) 4   (B) 32
(C) 16   (D) 40

7 The diagram shows some of the factors of 60.

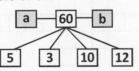

What are the possible values of a and b?

(A) a = 2, b = 16   (B) a = 4, b = 20
(C) a = 6, b = 25   (D) a = 8, b = 30

8 From the given diagram, what is the value of p + q + r?

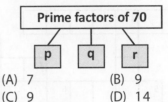

(A) 7   (B) 9
(C) 9   (D) 14

9 The given figure shows some of the factors of 156.

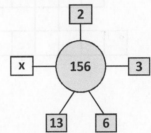

What is the value of x?

(A) 16   (B) 8
(C) 15   (D) 39

10 The figure given shows 5 numbers.

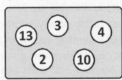

Which of the 5 numbers are the prime factors of 130?

(A) 2 and 3   (B) 10 and 13
(C) 2 and 13   (D) 3 and 10

✧ ✧ ✧

CROSSWORD

1. Large Numbers

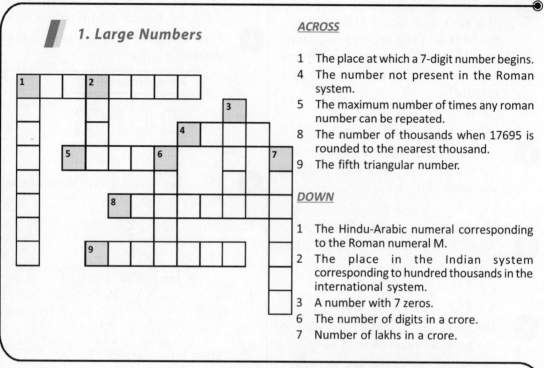

ACROSS

1 The place at which a 7-digit number begins.
4 The number not present in the Roman system.
5 The maximum number of times any roman number can be repeated.
8 The number of thousands when 17695 is rounded to the nearest thousand.
9 The fifth triangular number.

DOWN

1 The Hindu-Arabic numeral corresponding to the Roman numeral M.
2 The place in the Indian system corresponding to hundred thousands in the international system.
3 A number with 7 zeros.
6 The number of digits in a crore.
7 Number of lakhs in a crore.

2. Factors and Multiples

ACROSS

3 The factor of a number the sum of whose digits is divisible by 9.
4 The smallest factor of any number.
7 The factor of a number ending in zero.
9 The method of breaking up of composite number into their factors.
10 The highest common factor of 12 and 18.

DOWN

1 The rules that help us find the numbers that divide a given number exactly.
2 The numbers (except 1), that have only two factors.
5 The lowest common multiple of 10 and 20.
6 The largest factor of 20.
8 The least prime number.

Fractions

◆ **Fraction:**

A fraction is a part of whole. Fraction $= \dfrac{\text{Numerator}}{\text{Denominator}}$

In $\dfrac{6}{7}$, 6 is called numerator and 7 is called denominator.

The denominator denotes the number of equal parts the whole is divided into.

The numerator denotes the number of parts considered of the whole.

◆ **Types of Fractions:**

Like fractions: Fractions with same denominators.

e.g., $\dfrac{4}{5}, \dfrac{6}{5}, \dfrac{3}{5}$ etc.,

Unlike fractions: Fractions with different denominators.

e.g., $\dfrac{1}{2}, \dfrac{6}{8}, \dfrac{9}{4}$ etc.,

Proper fractions: Fractions in which the denominator is greater than the numerator.

e.g., $\dfrac{2}{9}, \dfrac{5}{6}, \dfrac{2}{3}$ etc.,

Improper fractions: Fractions in which the numerator is greater than the denominator.

e.g., $\dfrac{9}{2}, \dfrac{6}{5}, \dfrac{3}{2}$ etc.,

Mixed Number: A number with a whole number part and a fractional part is called a mixed number

e.g., $1\dfrac{1}{2}, 2\dfrac{1}{3}, 3\dfrac{1}{4}$ etc.,

◆ **Conversion of an improper fraction to a mixed number:**

e.g., Convert $\dfrac{13}{5}$ into a mixed number.

Solution: Divide $\dfrac{13}{5}$ and write in the form of $Q\dfrac{R}{D}$, where Q = Quotient, R = Remainder and D = Denominator (Divisor).

$$\begin{array}{r} 5)\ 13\ (2 \\ \underline{10} \\ 3 \end{array}$$

(D) ... (Q) ... (R)

$$\therefore \ \frac{13}{5} = 2\frac{3}{5}$$

♦ **Conversion of a mixed number to an improper fraction:**

e.g., Convert $3\frac{1}{4}$ into an improper fraction.

Solution: Comparing $3\frac{1}{4}$ with $Q\frac{R}{D}$, $Q = 3$, $R = 1$ and $D = 4$.

∴ The required improper fraction

$$= \frac{Q \times D + R}{D} = \frac{3 \times 4 + 1}{4} = \frac{13}{4}$$

♦ **Equivalent fractions:**

All fractions that have the same value are called equivalent fractions. Equivalent fractions of a given fraction are obtained by multiplying or dividing both numerator and denominator by the same number.

e.g., $\frac{1}{2}, \frac{5}{10}, \frac{11}{22}$ etc.,

If the cross products of two fractions are equal, they are equivalent.

e.g., (a) $\frac{3}{4}, \frac{75}{100}$

$$\frac{3}{4} \quad \frac{75}{100}$$

$3 \times 100 = 300$ and $75 \times 4 = 300$

is equivalent to $\frac{75}{100}$.

e.g., (b) $\frac{1}{5}, \frac{2}{3}$

$$\frac{1}{5} \quad \frac{2}{3}$$

$1 \times 3 = 3$ and $2 \times 5 = 10$

$3 \neq 10$

$\therefore \frac{1}{5}$ is not equivalent to $\frac{2}{3}$.

♦ **Simplification of fractions:**

Reducing a fraction to its lowest terms is called simplifying the fraction. Dividing the numerator and the denominator of a fraction by a factor common to both of them reduces it into its lowest terms.

A fraction is said to be in its lowest terms if its numerator and denominator have no common factor other than 1.

A fraction can be reduced to its lowest terms by cancelling the factors common to both numerator and denominator.

Lowest terms of a fraction can be found by dividing the numerator and denominator by their H.C.F.

e.g., Find the lowest terms of $\dfrac{18}{30}$.

Solution: The H.C.F. of 18 and 30 is 6.

$$\therefore \frac{18}{30} = \frac{18 \div 6}{30 \div 6} = \frac{3}{5}$$

> *Note:* **3 and 5 have no common factor other than 1.**

◆ **Comparing fractions:**

Among the like fractions, a fraction with greater numerator is the greater fraction. To compare unlike fractions, first convert them into equivalent fractions and then compare them.

While comparing fractions with the same numerators, the fraction with greater denominator is smaller.

Ordering fractions:

Ascending order: Fractions written in order from the smallest to the greatest are said to be in ascending order.

e.g., $\dfrac{1}{5}, \dfrac{1}{3}, \dfrac{1}{2}$ are fractions in ascending order.

Descending order: Fractions written in order from the greatest to the smallest are said to be in descending order.

e.g., $\dfrac{1}{2}, \dfrac{1}{4}, \dfrac{1}{5}$ are fractions in descending order.

◆ **Addition of like fractions:**

Add the numerators and write the sum on the same denominator.

e.g., $\dfrac{7}{8} + \dfrac{3}{8} + \dfrac{12}{8} = \dfrac{7 + 3 + 12}{8} = \dfrac{22}{8} = \dfrac{11}{4} = 2\dfrac{3}{4}$

◆ **Addition of unlike fractions:**

Convert the unlike fractions into like fractions with the common denominator (which is the L.C.M. of given denominators). Then add the numerators and write the sum on the same denominator.

e.g., $\dfrac{3}{5} + \dfrac{2}{3} = \dfrac{3 \times 3 + 2 \times 5}{15} = \dfrac{9 + 10}{15} = \dfrac{19}{15} = 1\dfrac{4}{15}$

Two mixed numbers can be added by adding whole numbers and fractions separately.

e.g., $2\dfrac{1}{3} + 3\dfrac{1}{4} = (2 + 3) + \left(\dfrac{1}{3} + \dfrac{1}{4}\right)$

$= 5 + \left(\dfrac{4 + 3}{12}\right) = 5\dfrac{7}{12}$

If the sum of two fractions is not in lowest terms, it must be reduced to the lowest terms.

◆ **Subtraction of fractions:**

Like fractions are subtracted by finding the difference of numerators.

e.g., $\dfrac{7}{15} - \dfrac{3}{15} = \dfrac{7 - 3}{15} = \dfrac{4}{15}$

Unlike fractions are converted to like fractions and then subtracted.

e.g., $\dfrac{9}{4} - \dfrac{3}{2} = \dfrac{18 - 12}{8} = \dfrac{6}{8} = \dfrac{3}{4}$

If the difference of two fractions is not in its lowest terms, it must be reduced to the lowest terms.

◆ **Multiplication of fractions:**

To get the product of a fraction and a whole number, multiply the numerator of the fraction with the whole number. Factors common to numerator and denominator can be cancelled.

e.g., $\dfrac{1}{2} \times 5 = \dfrac{5}{2}$

To get the product of two fractions, numerators and denominators are multiplied separately. Factors common to numerator and denominator are cancelled.

e.g., $\dfrac{1}{3} \times \dfrac{2}{5} = \dfrac{1 \times 2}{3 \times 5} = \dfrac{2}{15}$

When a fraction is multiplied by 1, the product is the fraction itself.

e.g., $\dfrac{3}{4} \times 1 = \dfrac{3}{4}$

When a fraction is multiplied by 0, the product is 0.

e.g., $\dfrac{2}{3} \times 0 = 0$

◆ **Finding the fraction of a number:**

To find the fraction of a quantity, the fraction and the number (quantity) are multiplied and simplified.

e.g., $\dfrac{1}{3}$ of ₹ 90 = $\dfrac{1}{3}$ × ₹ 90 = ₹ 30

◆ **Reciprocal or multiplicative inverse:**

Interchanging the numerator and denominator of a fraction results in its reciprocal.

e.g., $\dfrac{3}{2}$ is the reciprocal of $\dfrac{2}{3}$.

> **Note:** Two numbers are the multiplicative inverses of each other if their product is 1.

◆ **Division of fractions:**

Dividing a fraction by another fraction is to multiply the fraction by the reciprocal of the other.

e.g., $\dfrac{2}{3} \div \dfrac{6}{8} = \dfrac{2}{3} \times \dfrac{8}{6} = \dfrac{8}{3 \times 3} = \dfrac{8}{9}$

When a fraction is divided by 1, the quotient is the fraction itself.

e.g., $\dfrac{3}{4} \div 1 = \dfrac{3}{4}$

When 1 is divided by a fraction, the quotient is the reciprocal of the fraction.

e.g., $1 \div \dfrac{3}{4} = \dfrac{4}{3}$

When 0 is divided by a fraction, the quotient is 0.

e.g., $0 \div \dfrac{3}{6} = 0$

> **Note:** Division of a fraction by 0 is not defined as division by 0 is not defined.

When a fraction is multiplied by its reciprocal, the product is 1.

e.g., $\dfrac{3}{4} \times \dfrac{4}{3} = 1$

When a fraction is divided by itself, the quotient is 1.

e.g., $\dfrac{2}{3} \div \dfrac{2}{3} = 1$

Multiple Choice Questions

1. Find an equivalent fraction of $\frac{14}{35}$.

    (A) $\frac{27}{70}$ (B) $\frac{28}{35}$

    (C) $\frac{70}{175}$ (D) $\frac{70}{350}$

2. Observe the fractions given in the box.

    Which symbol must be placed in the box to make the statement correct?

    (A) <   (B) >
    (C) =   (D) Either (B) or (C)

3. Which of the following improper fractions is equivalent to $15\frac{2}{7}$?

    (A) $\frac{15}{14}$ (B) $\frac{107}{7}$

    (C) $\frac{30}{7}$ (D) $\frac{37}{7}$

4. Which mixed number is equal to $\frac{45}{14}$?

    (A) $14\frac{3}{14}$ (B) $3\frac{1}{14}$

    (C) $3\frac{3}{14}$ (D) $14\frac{1}{3}$

5. What is the sum of $\frac{5}{13}$, $\frac{11}{13}$ and $\frac{13}{13}$?

    (A) $14\frac{1}{13}$ (B) 1

    (C) $3\frac{2}{13}$ (D) $2\frac{3}{13}$

6. By what number is $\frac{19}{25}$ lesser than $\frac{27}{25}$?

    (A) $\frac{8}{25}$ (B) $\frac{5}{25}$

    (C) $\frac{6}{25}$ (D) $\frac{9}{25}$

7. What is the sum obtained when $\frac{8}{4}$, $\frac{9}{6}$ and $1\frac{3}{5}$ are added?

    (A) $5\frac{1}{10}$ (B) $\frac{59}{60}$

    (C) $5\frac{1}{30}$ (D) $\frac{59}{120}$

8. Find the difference obtained when $\frac{9}{40}$ is subtracted from $\frac{23}{40}$.

    (A) $\frac{25}{40}$ (B) $\frac{14}{40}$

    (C) $\frac{31}{40}$ (D) $\frac{32}{40}$

9. Which of the following is a proper fraction?

    (A) $\frac{4}{3}$ (B) $\frac{16}{9}$

    (C) $\frac{28}{15}$ (D) $\frac{11}{23}$

10. How is five-eighteenths written?

    (A) $\frac{5}{19}$ (B) $\frac{8}{15}$

    (C) $\frac{5}{18}$ (D) $\frac{18}{5}$

11 Observe the given figures.

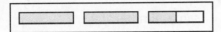

What fraction does the shaded part in the figures represent?

(A) $2\dfrac{1}{2}$ (B) $\dfrac{5}{4}$

(C) $2\dfrac{1}{5}$ (D) $\dfrac{6}{5}$

12 What is the reciprocal of $4\dfrac{2}{3}$?

(A) $4\dfrac{3}{2}$ (B) $\dfrac{14}{3}$

(C) $\dfrac{3}{14}$ (D) $2\dfrac{4}{3}$

13 Find the product of $1\dfrac{1}{3}$, $3\dfrac{1}{4}$ and $\dfrac{7}{8}$.

(A) $3\dfrac{5}{24}$ (B) $3\dfrac{19}{24}$

(C) $3\dfrac{1}{24}$ (D) $19\dfrac{3}{7}$

14 Raju scored 8 marks in a maths test for 15 marks. How is Raju's marks represented as a fraction of maximum marks of the test?

(A) $\dfrac{15}{8}$ (B) $\dfrac{23}{18}$

(C) $\dfrac{8}{23}$ (D) $\dfrac{8}{15}$

15 Identify the largest fraction among the following.

(A) $\dfrac{29}{30}$ (B) $\dfrac{29}{23}$

(C) $\dfrac{29}{27}$ (D) $\dfrac{29}{25}$

16 Gopal reads $\dfrac{3}{5}$ of a book. He has still 80 pages to be read to complete reading the book. How many pages are there in the book?

(A) 200   (B) 100

(C) 400   (D) 300

17 Ravi had $\dfrac{5}{6}$ of a cake. He ate $\dfrac{2}{3}$ of it. What part of the cake is remaining?

(A) $\dfrac{4}{9}$ (B) $\dfrac{5}{9}$

(C) $\dfrac{10}{18}$ (D) $\dfrac{1}{6}$

18 A family consumes $3\dfrac{1}{2}$ litres of milk every day. How many litres of milk did the family consume in February 2013?

(A) 91   (B) 28

(C) 56   (D) 98

19 What is the product obtained when a fraction is multiplied by its reciprocal?

(A) 0

(B) 1

(C) Reciprocal fraction

(D) The fraction itself

20 What is the sum of the reciprocals of 9 and $\dfrac{2}{9}$?

(A) $(4 \times 11) + 18$
(B) $(4 \times 8) + 11$

(C) $4\dfrac{11}{18}$

(D) $11\dfrac{4}{18}$

21 Observe the number line given.

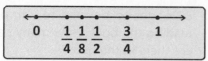

Which fraction represented on the number line is in a wrong place?

(A) $\dfrac{1}{2}$ (B) $\dfrac{1}{8}$

(C) $\dfrac{1}{4}$ (D) $\dfrac{3}{4}$

22 Which fraction shows the part of the circle that is shaded?

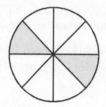

(A) $\dfrac{1}{8}$ (B) $\dfrac{1}{4}$

(C) $\dfrac{1}{16}$ (D) $\dfrac{2}{6}$

23 Which of the following is the same as $11\dfrac{3}{5} \times 15$?

(A) $11 \times \dfrac{45}{5}$ (B) $55 \times \dfrac{45}{5}$

(C) $165 \times \dfrac{45}{5}$ (D) 58×3

24 How many tenths are there in $2\dfrac{4}{5}$?

(A) 8   (B) 14

(C) 24   (D) 28

25 $\dfrac{2}{5}$ of a number is 48. What is $\dfrac{3}{5}$ of the same number?

(A) 50   (B) 72
(C) 56   (D) 78

26 There are 60 insects in a miniature garden. 12 of the insects are ladybirds and $\dfrac{1}{4}$ of them are butterflies. The rest of the insects are ants. What fraction of the insects in the garden are ants?

(A) $\dfrac{1}{3}$ (B) $\dfrac{27}{20}$

(C) $\dfrac{11}{20}$ (D) $\dfrac{3}{4}$

27 Find the fraction greater than $\dfrac{7}{8}$.

(A) $\dfrac{2}{3}$ (B) $\dfrac{5}{8}$

(C) $\dfrac{9}{11}$ (D) $\dfrac{11}{12}$

28 The mass of a flower pot is $13\dfrac{1}{3}$ kg.

The mass of a packet of soil is $4\dfrac{1}{5}$ kg heavier than the flower pot. What is the total mass of the flower pot and the packet of soil?

(A) $17\dfrac{8}{15}$ kg   (B) $21\dfrac{11}{15}$ kg

(C) $22\dfrac{7}{15}$ kg   (D) $30\dfrac{13}{15}$ kg

29 Study the pattern given.

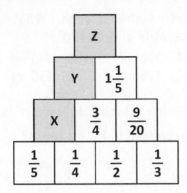

What is the value of Z?

(A) $1\dfrac{17}{60}$

(B) $1\dfrac{7}{12}$

(C) $2\dfrac{47}{60}$

(D) $3\dfrac{47}{60}$

30 John had some pencils. $\dfrac{3}{5}$ of them were red and the rest were green. He gave $\dfrac{2}{3}$ of the red pencils and $\dfrac{1}{4}$ of the green pencils to his sister. If he had 80 pencils left, how many pencils did he have at first?

(A) 240   (B) 40
(C) 160   (D) 200

31 What is 35 seconds as a fraction of 1 minute?

(A) $\dfrac{1}{4}$

(B) $\dfrac{1}{35}$

(C) $\dfrac{7}{12}$

(D) $\dfrac{7}{20}$

32 What is the missing number in the box?

$$\dfrac{7}{10} - \dfrac{2}{5} + \dfrac{1}{2} = \dfrac{4}{\boxed{?}}$$

(A) 5   (B) 10
(C) 13   (D) 20

33 Bhanu bought $\dfrac{2}{3}$ m of ribbon to wrap 5 presents. He used the same amount of ribbon for each present. What was the length of ribbon used for each present?

(A) $\dfrac{2}{17}$ m

(B) $\dfrac{2}{15}$ m

(C) $\dfrac{7}{15}$ m

(D) $\dfrac{3}{17}$ m

34 $\dfrac{2}{3}$ of a number is smaller than thrice the same number by 49. What is the number?

(A) 14   (B) 35
(C) 21   (D) 28

35 Jamuna bought $\dfrac{7}{8}$ m of cloth to make a doll dress. She used $\dfrac{2}{5}$ of the cloth. What length of the cloth is left?

(A) $\dfrac{21}{40}$ m

(B) $\dfrac{19}{40}$ m

(C) $\dfrac{7}{20}$ m

(D) $\dfrac{7}{10}$ m

36 Study the pattern of fractions.

$$\dfrac{3}{4},\ 1\dfrac{4}{5},\ 2\dfrac{5}{6},\ \boxed{?},\ 4\dfrac{7}{8}$$

How is the missing fraction expressed as a mixed fraction?

(A) $6\dfrac{3}{7}$

(B) $7\dfrac{3}{5}$

(C) $3\dfrac{6}{7}$

(D) $6\dfrac{1}{7}$

37 What is the simplest form of 55 minutes as a fraction of $2\dfrac{1}{4}$ hours?

(A) $\dfrac{10}{27}$ (B) $\dfrac{55}{59}$

(C) $\dfrac{12}{30}$ (D) $\dfrac{11}{27}$

38 12 penguins shared $\dfrac{6}{7}$ kg of fish equally. How much fish did each one receive?

(A) $\dfrac{1}{4}$ kg   (B) $\dfrac{1}{14}$ kg

(C) $\dfrac{1}{11}$ kg   (D) $\dfrac{4}{11}$ kg

39 What is the value of $\dfrac{14}{15} \div 6$ in its lowest terms?

(A) $\dfrac{7}{45}$ (B) $\dfrac{7}{15}$

(C) $\dfrac{14}{15}$ (D) $\dfrac{14}{90}$

40 After selling $4\dfrac{4}{5}$ kg of salt, a shopkeeper had $4\dfrac{7}{10}$ kg of salt left. How much salt did he have at first?

(A) $\dfrac{95}{18}$ kg   (B) $\dfrac{25}{33}$ kg

(C) $9\dfrac{1}{2}$ kg   (D) $\dfrac{1}{10}$ kg

41 A flask holds $\dfrac{3}{4}\,l$ of coffee. It is poured into 6 similar cups. What is the capacity of each cup?

(A) 250 ml (B) 375 ml
(C) 125 ml (D) 150 ml

42 Which of the following is $\dfrac{16}{48}$ expressed in lowest terms?

(A) $\dfrac{8}{24}$ (B) $\dfrac{4}{12}$

(C) $\dfrac{1}{3}$ (D) $\dfrac{2}{6}$

43 Monica had $3\dfrac{1}{2}$ m of ribbon and Jaya had $\dfrac{2}{5}$ m of ribbon. How much more ribbon did Monica have?

(A) $\dfrac{3}{5}$ m   (B) $\dfrac{5}{3}$ m

(C) $3\dfrac{3}{10}$ m   (D) $3\dfrac{1}{10}$ m

Previous Contest Questions

1 A jar can hold 6 l of water. It can fill 8 mugs when it is full. How many litres of water can each mug hold?

(A) $\dfrac{3}{4}\,l$ (B) $1\dfrac{1}{3}\,l$

(C) 14 l (D) 48 l

2 Manish had ₹ 45. He spent $\dfrac{3}{5}$ of it on a birthday present. How much had he left?

(A) ₹ 27   (B) ₹ 18
(C) ₹ 9   (D) ₹ 5

3 What must be added to $2\dfrac{2}{5}$ to give

$3\dfrac{3}{10}$?

(A) $\dfrac{9}{10}$ (B) $1\dfrac{1}{5}$

(C) $\dfrac{5}{6}$ (D) $5\dfrac{7}{10}$

4 Mona is $\dfrac{1}{4}$ m shorter than Aarti. If

Mona is $1\dfrac{3}{8}$ m tall, how tall is Aarti?

(A) $1\dfrac{1}{8}$ m   (B) $1\dfrac{1}{6}$ m

(C) $1\dfrac{1}{4}$ m   (D) $1\dfrac{5}{8}$ m

5 2 boys took a test. Pavan scored $\dfrac{4}{5}$ of

what Prateek had scored. If Pavan scored 76 marks, what was their total marks?

(A) 165 marks   (B) 171 marks
(C) 181 marks   (D) 190 marks

6 The capacity of a cylindrical tank is

$32\,l$. It is $\dfrac{4}{5}$ full of water. A quarter of

this volume of water is poured into a pail. How much water is left in the cyclindrical tank?

(A) $15\dfrac{1}{9}\,l$ (B) $19\dfrac{3}{5}\,l$

(C) $19\dfrac{1}{5}\,l$ (D) $15\dfrac{3}{5}\,l$

7 Study the following equation.

$$2 \times \boxed{?} = \dfrac{2}{5} \div 13$$

What is the missing fraction in the box?

(A) $\dfrac{3}{65}$ (B) $\dfrac{1}{65}$

(C) $\dfrac{7}{65}$ (D) $\dfrac{9}{65}$

8 Which of the following is $1\dfrac{1}{2}$ years as

a fraction of 54 months?

(A) $\dfrac{2}{3}$ (B) $\dfrac{1}{4}$

(C) $\dfrac{3}{4}$ (D) $\dfrac{1}{3}$

9 The sum of the numerator and the denominator of a fraction is 67. When 31 is added to the denominator, the

fraction becomes $\dfrac{3}{11}$. What was the

original fraction?

(A) $\dfrac{23}{47}$ (B) $\dfrac{20}{43}$

(C) $\dfrac{21}{46}$ (D) $\dfrac{21}{61}$

10 Observe the given equation.

$$\dfrac{5}{6} \times 15 = \dfrac{\boxed{?}}{12} \times 30$$

Identify the missing number in the box.

(A) 15   (B) 40
(C) 25   (D) 5

✧ ✧ ✧

Decimals

Synopsis

♦ **Decimal numbers:** Fractions with 10, 100, 1000 or any multiple of 10 are called decimal numbers.

♦ **Decimal numbers have two parts:**

(a) Whole number (Part which is on the left hand side to the decimal point)

(b) Decimal part (Part which is on the right hand side to the decimal point)

e.g., In the decimal number 5.789, 5 is the whole number part and 789 is decimal part, read as five point seven eight nine.

♦ **Place value Chart of decimal numbers:**

Thousands	Hundreds	Tens	Ones	Tenths	Hundredths	Thousandths
1000	100	10	1	$\dfrac{1}{10}$	$\dfrac{1}{100}$	$\dfrac{1}{1000}$

As we move from right to left, the value of digits increases by 10 times.

As we move from left to right, its value decreases by 10 times.

♦ **Expanded form of decimals:**

To express a number in expanded form, write each digit of the number with its corresponding place value with a + sign between them.

e.g., 45.459 = 4 tens + 5 ones + 4 tenths + 5 hundredths + 9 thousandths

$$= 40 + 5 + \frac{4}{10} + \frac{5}{100} + \frac{9}{1000}$$

Adding any number of zeroes to the right of a significant digit in the decimal part does not change its value.

e.g., 3.4 is the same as 3.40 or 3.400 etc., whereas 3.04 is not the same as 3.004 etc. The places of the digits are to be taken into consideration.

♦ **Converting Decimals into Fractions:**

(i) To convert a decimal number into a fraction, write the decimal number without the decimal point as the numerator of the fraction.

(ii) Write the denominator of the fraction by inserting as many zeroes on the right of 1 as the number of decimal places in the given decimal number.

(iii) Simplify the fraction if possible, i.e., write the fraction in the lowest terms.

e.g., $78.59 = \dfrac{7859}{100}$

◆ **Like and unlike decimals:** The decimal numbers having the same number of decimal places (digits after the decimal point) are called Like Decimals.

e.g., 20.89, 4.02, 45.94 and 0.23 are called like decimals.

The decimal numbers having different number of decimal places (digits after the decimal point) are called Unlike Decimals.

Unlike decimals may or may not be equivalent decimals.

e.g., 12.455, 1.23, 78.5 and 42.555 are unlike decimals.

◆ **Equivalent Decimals:** The decimals obtained by multiplying and dividing a given decimal number by multiples of 10 are called equivalent decimals.

e.g., 0.7, 0.70, 0.700 etc.,

◆ **Converting unlike decimals into like decimals:**

To convert unlike decimals to like decimals, find the number in which the largest number of decimal places is present, and change the other decimals into their equivalent decimals, with the same number of decimal places as the largest number of decimal places.

e.g., 50.36, 459.2656

459.2656 has four decimal places.

50.36 has two decimal places.

50.3600 is an equivalent decimal for 50.36.

Hence, 50.3600, 459.2656 are like decimals.

◆ **Comparing two decimal numbers:**

We can compare two like decimals just as we compare two whole numbers ignoring the decimal point.

For comparing two unlike decimals, first convert them into like decimals and then compare.

◆ **Addition of Decimals:**

(i) Addition of decimals is similar to addition without decimal, in which we place the addends in such a way that the decimal point of all the numbers are in the same column.

(ii) Add the numbers ignoring the decimal point.

(iii) Place the decimal point in the sum directly under the decimal point of all the addends.

(iv) If numbers are unlike decimals convert them into like decimals and then add.

e.g., What is the sum of 450.36, 45.56 and 12.369?

Solution:
```
    450.360
     45.560
  + 12.369
  ─────────
    508.289
  ─────────
```

◆ **Subtraction of Decimals:**

(i) Place the larger number first and the smaller number below it in such a way that the decimal point of both the numbers are in the same column.

(ii) Subtract the number (ignoring the decimal point) as in the case of whole numbers.

(iii) Place the decimal point in the result directly under the decimal point of the two given decimals.

e.g., Subtract 22.89 from 78.56.
```
    78.56
  - 22.89
  ────────
    55.67
  ────────
```

Note:

(a) **For addition or subtraction of decimals ensure that the digits with the same place value are arranged one below the other.**

(b) **Find equivalent decimals if needed, by adding 0s after the last significant digit as it does not change the value of the given decimals.**

◆ **Multiplication of decimals:**

(a) **Multiplication of a decimal number by a whole number**

e.g., Find the product of 45.98 and 8.

Step 1: Multiply the given numbers as whole numbers ignoring the decimal point.
```
     4598
   ×    8
   ───────
    36784
   ───────
```

Step 2: In the product, place the decimal point after so many digits from the right as the number of decimal places in the multiplicand.

In 45.98, the number of decimal places is 2. So, in the product 36784, place the decimal point after 2 places from the right.

Thus, 45.98 × 8 = 367.84

> **Note:**
>
> **Multiplication of a whole number by a decimal number is the same as multiplication of a decimal number by a whole number.**

(b) Multiplication of a decimal number by a decimal number

e.g., Find the product of 45.98 and 8.5.

Step 1: Multiply the given numbers as whole numbers ignoring the decimal point.

$$
\begin{array}{r}
4598 \\
\times 85 \\
\hline
22990 \\
36784\times \\
\hline
390830 \\
\end{array}
$$

Step 2: In the product, place the decimal point after so many digits from the right as the sum of number of decimal places in the multiplicand and the multiplier.

Total number of decimal places in the multiplicand and the multiplier is 2 + 1 = 3.

So, in the product 390830, place the decimal point after 3 digits from the right.

Thus, 45.98 x 8.5 = 390.830 = 390.83

(The last 0 can be ignored as it does not alter the value of the decimal.)

◆ **Division of decimal numbers:**

(a) Division of a decimal number by a whole number

Divide the decimal number by the whole number as usual division of whole numbers.

After the whole number part is divided, place a decimal point in the quotient before dividing the decimal part. Continue the division till the remainder is zero or upto a desired number of decimal places.

If the whole number part of the decimal number is 0, first place a 0 and a decimal point beside it in the quotient. Divide as usual until zero is obtained as remainder or upto a desired number of decimal places.

Shortcut to multiply a decimal number by multiples of 10:

Decimal number	Multiple of 10	Number of places the decimal is shifted right	Product
2.481	10	1	24.81
2.481	100	2	248.1
2.481	1000	3	2481
2.481	10000	4	24810

Note:

When a decimal number is multiplied by multiples of 10, the decimal point shifts right by the number of places as the number of zeroes in the multiple of 10.

Shortcut to divide a decimal number by multiples of 10:

Decimal number	Multiple of 10	Number of places the decimal is shifted left	Quotient
788.6	10	1	78.86
788.6	100	2	7.886
788.6	1000	3	0.7886
788.6	10000	4	0.07886

Note:

When a decimal number is divided by multiples of 10, the decimal point shifts left by the number of places as the number of zeroes in the multiple of 10.

◆ **Rounding off and Estimation:**

To round off a decimal number to 2 decimal places, we consider the digit in the third place, (thousandths place). If it is < 5, we round the number down. If it is > = 5, we round the number up.

e.g., Round off 43.256 to 2 decimal places.

In 43.256, the thousandths digit 6 > 5. So, we round it up as 43.26 to 2 decimal places.

The same procedure is carried out for rounding off to 1 decimal place.

e.g., 52.14 is 52.1 when rounded to 1 decimal place, as 4 < 5.

To round off a decimal number to the nearest whole number, we consider the tenths place and round it up or down as usual.

To check whether the answers are reasonable, we estimate by rounding off the decimal to the nearest whole number.

e.g., $3.42 \times 15 \approx 3 \times 15 = 45$

Multiple Choice Questions

1. Which decimal number is equivalent to $\frac{78}{100}$?

   (A) 0.78   (B) 78.00
   (C) 0.078   (D) 7.8

2. How is 3 tenths 5 thousandths written in decimals?

   (A) 35.00   (B) 0.35
   (C) 3.5   (D) 0.305

3. What is the sum of 0.3, 0.03 and 0.003?

   (A) 0.999   (B) 0.393
   (C) 0.636   (D) 0.333

4. What is the difference of 32 and 27.091?

   (A) 30.791   (B) 5.909
   (C) 4.909   (D) 3.909

5. What is the product of 78.12 and 1.5?

   (A) 117.81   (B) 117.18
   (C) 117.32   (D) 117.80

6. Find the quotient obtained when 125.625 is divided by 0.5.

   (A) 251.25   (B) 2512.5
   (C) 25125   (D) 25.125

7. How is 5 thousandths written as a decimal number?

   (A) 0.05   (B) 0.005
   (C) 5.000   (D) 0.056

8. Identify the decimal number form of 2 tens 6 thousandths.

   (A) 20.6   (B) 20.06
   (C) 210.6000   (D) 20.006

9. Find the quotient in the division given in the box.

   $$9.826 \div 10$$

   (A) 98.26   (B) 982.6
   (C) 0.09826   (D) 0.9826

10. Evaluate the product in the box.

    $$0.05 \times 0.09 \times 5$$

    (A) 0.025   (B) 0.225
    (C) 0.005   (D) 0.0225

11. Study the following sum.

    $$18.0006 + 14.005 + 12.34 = \boxed{?}$$

    Find the missing number.

    (A) 45.3356   (B) 45.3255
    (C) 44.3456   (D) 44.3356

12. If $2805 \div 2.55 = 1100$, find the quotient of $280.5 \div 25.5$.

    (A) 1.1   (B) 1.01
    (C) 0.11   (D) 11

13. How is 0.23 represented as a vulgar fraction?

    (A) $\frac{7}{30}$ (B) $\frac{23}{100}$

    (C) $\frac{23}{90}$ (D) $\frac{7}{90}$

14. Find the value of $\left(\frac{0.1}{0.01} + \frac{0.01}{0.1} \right)$.

    (A) 10.1   (B) 1.10
    (C) 1.01   (D) 10.01

15. Given 0.111 is approximately equal to $\frac{1}{9}$, what is the approximate value of 0.777?

    (A) $\frac{5}{9}$ (B) $\frac{7}{9}$

    (C) $\frac{2}{9}$ (D) $\frac{1}{9}$

16 The cost of 15 pens is ₹ 148.50. What is the cost of 1 pen?

(A) ₹ 12.80   (B) ₹ 8.90
(C) ₹ 10.90   (D) ₹ 9.90

17 What is the cost of 30.5 litres of milk at the rate of ₹ 7.50 per litre?

(A) ₹ 225.75   (B) ₹ 223.75
(C) ₹ 228.75   (D) ₹ 232.75

18 The sum of two numbers is 31.021. If one of them is 11.56, find the other.

(A) 19.461   (B) 17.461
(C) 18.641   (D) 19.561

19 A shopkeeper sold 12.750 kg of sugar on a day. On the next day he sold 38.250 kg of sugar. On the third day he sold 50.500 kg of sugar. How much of sugar in all did the shopkeeper sell?

(A) 100 kg   (B) 101.5 kg
(C) 102.5 kg   (D) 101 kg

20 What type of decimals are the numbers given?

16.37	18.97
12.26	21.48

(A) Like decimal numbers
(B) Unlike decimal numbers
(C) Equivalent decimal numbers
(D) Estimated decimal numbers

21 Study the decimal number line given.

6.37   6.5   P   Q   R   7.02

What is the value of P + Q − R?

(A) 5.59   (B) 6.47
(C) 6.5   (D) 20.27

22 What is the value of 11.047 rounded off to the nearest tenth?

(A) 11.0   (B) 11.1
(C) 11.2   (D) 12.04

23 What is the number obtained on rounding off 32.4 to the nearest ones?

(A) 30   (B) 32
(C) 33   (D) 35

24 Which one of the following is the best estimate for 9.85 × 23.099?

(A) 9 × 23   (B) 9 × 24
(C) 10 × 23   (D) 10 × 24

25 How many hundredths less than 5.47 is 5.07?

(A) 40   (B) 500
(C) 4000   (D) 4

26 How many hundredths more than 1.98 is 21 tenths?

(A) 21   (B) 15
(C) 1.2   (D) 12

27 What is the value of $\frac{7}{8}$ rounded off to 1 decimal place?

(A) 0.875   (B) 0.9
(C) 0.88   (D) 0.8

28 What is the value of

$$14 + \frac{8}{10} + \frac{108}{100} + \frac{345}{1000}?$$

(A) 16.225   (B) 15.262
(C) 16.252   (D) 16.255

29 65 hundredths of a number is 130. What is the number?

(A) 200   (B) 150
(C) 300   (D) 260

(30-31): A tank can hold 20.145 l of water. $\frac{3}{5}$ of the water in the tank is used for different purposes.

30 What amount of water is used?

(A) 4.029 l (B) 9.058 l
(C) 12.087 l (D) 60.435 l

31 What quantity of water is remaining in the tank?

(A) 8.185 l (B) 9.158 l

(C) 8.508 l (D) 8.058 l

32 What is the product when the sum of 1.048 and 3.162 is multiplied by 39?

(A) 4.21   (B) 43.21

(C) 124.36   (D) 164.19

33 A nylon string 18 m long is cut into equal pieces of 0.2 m each. How many equal pieces are obtained?

(A) 180   (B) 90

(C) 9   (D) 360

34 Which of the following decimal numbers has the greatest value?

(A) 0.109   (B) 0.19

(C) 0.11   (D) 0.101

35 A shopkeeper mixed 3.6 kg of grade-II cashew nuts in 0.75 kg of grade-I cashew nuts. He packed the mixture equally into 5 boxes. What is the mass of each box?

(A) 21.75 kg   (B) 4.35 kg

(C) 2.85 kg   (D) 0.87 kg

36 A coil of wire 12.948 m long is cut into 4 pieces. The length of 3 pieces is 3.085 m each. What is the length of the fourth piece?

(A) 2.693 m   (B) 3.693 m

(C) 5.693 m   (D) 4.693 m

37 Study the decimal numbers given in the box.

0.684	68.4	684	6.84
P	Q	R	S

Find the correct descending order of numbers.

(A) P, Q, R, S   (B) Q, R, P, S

(C) R, Q, S, P   (D) R, Q, P, S

38 The mass of a table is 29.437 kg. What is the approximate mass of 5 such tables?

(A) 145 kg   (B) 154 kg

(C) 150 kg   (D) 100 kg

Previous Contest Questions

1 The height of a wooden block is 12.28 cm. What is the approximate height of 14 similar blocks stacked on top of each other?

(A) 171 cm   (B) 168 cm

(C) 170 cm   (D) 171.92 cm

2 15 packets of rice each weighing 6.25 kg are repacked into packets weighing 4 kg. During the repacking, 1.75 kg of rice is lost. How many 4 kg packets of rice were obtained?

(A) 8   (B) 38

(C) 23.5   (D) 23

3 The cost of a pencil and an eraser is ₹ 0.70 Priya bought 3 pencils and 4 erasers and paid ₹ 2.40. How much do 2 pencils and 2 erasers cost?

(A) ₹ 3.40   (B) ₹ 2.50

(C) ₹ 1.40   (D) ₹ 1.10

4 20 cakes were baked using 74.4 kg of flour. How much flour is needed to bake 13 cakes?

(A) 48 kg   (B) 48.36 kg

(C) 51 kg   (D) 49 kg

5 Study the equation given.

$$7.8 + 2.4 \div 60 - 0.09 = R$$

Find the value of R rounded off to one decimal place.

(A) 7.8   (B) 7.75

(C) 7.7   (D) 8

6 Suman had to multiply 14.36 by 23. Instead, he added the two numbers. What is the difference between his answer and the actual answer?

(A) 291.92   (B) 292
(C) 293.92   (D) 292.92

7 In which place is the digit 7 in the number given?

$$645.7849$$

(A) Tenths   (B) Ones
(C) Hundredths   (D) Thousandths

8 Find the resulting decimal number when the given decimal expression is evaluated?

$$2 \times 0.5 + 9 \div 0.3 + 10 \times 0.92$$

(A) 33.0   (B) 40.2
(C) 6.0   (D) 31.2

9 Find the quotient of the given division.

$$\frac{17.28 \div 12}{3.6 \times 0.2}$$

(A) 0.2   (B) 2
(C) 20   (D) 0.02

10 What is the resultant of $0.3 \div 0.3 \times 3$?

(A) $\frac{1}{3}$ (B) 0.3

(C) $\frac{1}{0.3}$ (D) 3

✧ ✧ ✧

CROSSWORD

3. Fractions

ACROSS

ACROSS

1   The form of a fraction in which the only common factor of the numerator and denominator is one.
4   The numerator of a fraction with denominator 12, equivalent to 2/3.
5   The cross-products of equivalent fractions.
6   The numerator of the lowest terms of the fraction 14/50.
8   The method used to check the equivalence of two fractions.
9   The numerator of a unit fraction.
10 The product of a fraction and zero.

DOWN

2   The fractions obtained by multiplying or dividing the numerator and denominator of a fraction by the same number.
3   The number equivalent to an improper fraction.
7   Fraction having same denominator.

4. Decimals

ACROSS

2   Decimals with different number of decimal places.
4   10 hundredths
6   The number of zeros in the denominator and the number of decimal places.
7   5.3, 5.30, 5.300, 5.3000, ...
8   The method used to find the value of a unit price.

DOWN

1   Decimals with the same number of decimal places.
3   The shift by 3 places in the decimal point when a decimal number is divided by 1000.
5   The number of decimal places in the product and the sum of the number of decimal places in the factors.
9   The number of places, the decimal point shifts right when a decimal number is multiplied by 100.
10 The number of thousandths in a hundredth.

CHAPTER 5

Arithmetic

Synopsis

◆ **Percent:**

'Per cent' means 'for every hundred'.

Symbol for percentage is %.

◆ **Conversions:**

a) **Percentage to decimals:**

To convert a percentage to a decimal, divide the number by 100.

e.g., $68\% = \dfrac{68}{100} = 0.68$

b) **Decimal to percentage:**

To convert a decimal to a percentage, multiply the number by 100%.

e.g., $0.59 = 0.59 \times 100\% = 59\%$

c) **Percentage to fraction:**

To convert a percentage to a fraction, write the number with denominator 100 and reduce the fraction to its lowest terms.

e.g., $45\% = \dfrac{45}{100} = \dfrac{9}{20}$

d) **Fraction to percentage:**

To convert a fraction to a percentage, multiply one fraction with 100%

e.g., $\dfrac{9}{20} = \dfrac{9}{20} \times 100\% = 45\%$

e) **Finding the percent of a quantity:**

To find the percent of a quantity, multiply them and simplify.

e.g.,   30% of ₹ 100

$= \dfrac{30}{100} \times ₹\ 100 = ₹\ 30$

◆ **Average:**

$$\text{Average} = \frac{\text{The sum of quantities}}{\text{The number of quantities}}$$

◆ **Ratio:**

(a) The comparison of two quantities of the same kind by division gives their ratio.

(b) The two quantities compared are written with a : (colon) between them.

   e.g., a : b read as 'a is to b'.

(c) Ratio of two numbers can be thought of as a fraction and all the rules for operations with fractions can be used.

(d) Double, triple, four times, etc., can be expressed in ratio as 2 : 1, 3 : 1, 4 : 1, etc.

(e) A ratio can be expressed as a fraction.

   e.g., 2 : 5 is the same as $\frac{2}{5}$.

(f) In a ratio a : b, the first term 'a' is called the antecedent and the second term 'b' is called the consequent . The order of terms of a ratio is important i.e., 1 : 4 is not the same ratio as 4 : 1.

(g) To find the ratio of two like quantities, they should be changed into the same unit of measurement.

(h) While writing a ratio, co-prime numbers are generally used, that is, the ratio is often expressed in the lowest terms by cancelling the common factors from both the numbers.

(i) A ratio does not have any unit of measurement.

◆ **Speed, Distance and Time:**

$$\text{Speed} = \frac{\text{Distance}}{\text{Time}}$$

$$\text{Average speed} = \frac{\text{Total distance covered}}{\text{Total time taken}}$$

$$\text{Distance} = \text{Speed} \times \text{Time}$$

$$\text{Time} = \frac{\text{Distance}}{\text{Speed}}$$

◆ **Simple Interest:**

$$I = \frac{PTR}{100}, \text{ where } I = \text{Interest}, P = \text{Principal}, T = \text{Time}, R = \text{Rate per annum}$$

Amount $(A) = P + I \Rightarrow I = A - P$ and also $P = A - I$

◆ **Profit and Loss:**

(i) The price of an article is called its cost price denoted as C.P.

(ii) The price at which an article is sold is called its selling price denoted as S.P.

(iii) If the selling price is greater than the cost price, there is a gain/profit, which is equal to the difference of selling price and cost price.

∴ If S.P. > C.P., gain = S.P. – C.P.

a) S.P. = Gain + C.P.

b) C.P. = S.P. – Gain

(iv) If S.P. < C.P. there is a loss, which is equal to the difference of cost price and selling price.

∴ If S.P. < C.P., loss = C.P. – S.P.

a) C.P. = Loss + S.P

b) S.P. = C.P. – Loss

◆ **Percentage profit and percentage loss:**
Profit or loss is incurred on the cost price.

So, percentage profit = $\dfrac{\text{Profit}}{\text{C.P.}} \times 100\%$ and percentage loss = $\dfrac{\text{loss}}{\text{C.P.}} \times 100\%$.

Multiple Choice Questions   A B C D

1 How is 89% written?

(A) $\dfrac{89}{100}$ (B) $\dfrac{98}{100}$

(C) 8.9   (D) $8\dfrac{9}{100}$

2 What is the decimal for 79%?

(A) 7.9   (B) 0.79
(C) 79.00   (D) 1.79

3 What is the missing number?

| 0.97 is equal to _____ % |

(A) 9.7   (B) 9.71
(C) 97   (D) 0.97

4 Which of the following is 75% of 35 kg?

(A) 2625 kg   (B) 26.25 kg
(C) 262.5 kg   (D) 2.625 kg

5 Observe the following.

| 10% of ₹ 100 ☐ 50% of ₹ 10 |

Which symbol must be placed in the box?

(A) <   (B) =
(C) >   (D) Either (A) or (B)

6 10% of plants in a garden are pink rose plants, 30% are red rose plants, 40% are white rose plants and the remaining are jasmine plants. If there are 400 plants in the garden, how many jasmine plants are there in the garden?

(A) 320   (B) 80
(C) 400   (D) 160

7 Sudha scored 312 out of 450 marks. What is her percentage marks?

(A) 69%   (B) 69.4%
(C) 69.33%   (D) 69.5%

8 If 6 squares out of 32 are coloured on a board, what is the percentage of coloured squares?

(A) 1875%   (B) 1.875%
(C) 187.5%   (D) 18.75%

9 Rohan's mother gave him ₹ 300, out of which he spent 15% on stationery, 35% on eatables and saved the remaining amount. How much did Rohan save?

(A) ₹ 200   (B) ₹ 100
(C) ₹ 150   (D) ₹ 50

10 What percent of the squares on a chess board are black?

(A) 50%   (B) 60%
(C) 15%   (D) 75%

11 In a school there were 125 teachers out of whom 15 were maths teachers. Find the percentage of maths teachers.

(A) 12%   (B) 14%
(C) 15%   (D) 25%

12 Prashanth invests 65% in machinery, 20% in raw material and still has ₹ 1305 cash with him. Find his total investment.

(A) ₹ 8500   (B) ₹ 8700
(C) ₹ 6800   (D) ₹ 9600

13 If 37.5% of a number is 450, what is 87.5% of the same number?

(A) 825   (B) 1175
(C) 1050   (D) 1250

14 What percent of 270 kg is 108 kg?

(A) 40%   (B) 36%
(C) 30%   (D) 25%

15 Two numbers are respectively 20% and 50% more than the third number. What % is the first number of the second?

(A) 40%   (B) 50%
(C) 80%   (D) 70%

16 The salary of a man increased by 20%. If his new salary is ₹ 3000, what was his salary before the increase?

(A) ₹ 2000   (B) ₹ 2300
(C) ₹ 2400   (D) ₹ 2500

17 The average age of 6 students is 11 years. If two more students of ages 14 years and 16 years join, what will their average age be?

(A) 13 years   (B) 12 years

(C) $12\frac{1}{2}$ years   (D) $11\frac{1}{2}$ years

18 The average temperature of the first three days of a week is 27 °C and that of the next three days is 29 °C. If the weekly average is 28.5 °C, what is the temperature on the last day?

(A) 31.5 °C   (B) 28 °C
(C) 21 °C   (D) 42 °C

19 What is the average of 5, 0, 6, $\frac{1}{4}$ and $8\frac{3}{4}$?

(A) 1   (B) 2
(C) 3   (D) 4

20 What is the ratio of ₹ 3 and 60 paise?

(A) 1 : 20   (B) 5 : 1
(C) 1 : 2   (D) 20 : 1

21 In a class there are 50 boys and 30 girls. What is the ratio of number of boys to number of girls in the class?

(A) 80 : 50   (B) 3 : 5
(C) 5 : 3   (D) 50 : 80

22 What is the ratio of 0.12 kg and 180 g?

(A) 0.01 : 1.8   (B) 1 : 15
(C) 2 : 3   (D) 3 : 2

23 If ₹ 60 is divided into two parts in the ratio 2 : 3, what is the difference between those two parts?

(A) ₹ 10   (B) ₹ 12
(C) ₹ 5   (D) ₹ 14

24 Mala and Bala got 75 marks and 25 marks respectively in an examination. Find the ratio of the marks scored by Mala to the total marks obtained by both of them.

(A) 3 : 4   (B) 3 : 1
(C) 1 : 3   (D) 4 : 3

25 The ratio of the heights of A and B is 4 : 3. If B is 1.2 m tall, find the height of A.

(A) 0.9 m   (B) 1.8 m
(C) 1.6 m   (D) 1.7 m

26 If a car travels 150 km in 5 hours, what is its speed?

(A) 150 km/h   (B) 30 km/h
(C) 50 km/h   (D) 10 km/h

27 A student has to reach his school in 15 minutes. If the school is 800 metres away, at what speed should he walk?

(A) $\frac{800}{15}$ m/s   (B) $\frac{1}{15}$ m/s

(C) $\frac{8}{9}$ m/s   (D) $\frac{1}{9}$ m/s

28 A car travels at 45 km per hour. How much time will it take to cover 90 km?

(A) 1 hour   (B) 2 hours
(C) 3 hours   (D) 10 hours

29 A cycle travels at a speed of 45 km/h. How far will it travel in 36 minutes?

(A) 27 km   (B) 20 km
(C) 36 km   (D) 45 km

30 A boy runs at a speed of 8 m/s. How long does he take to cover a distance of 1 km?

(A) 100 sec   (B) 125 sec
(C) 12.5 hr   (D) 150 sec

31 If the sum of ₹ 415 amounts to 450, what is the interest earned?

(A) ₹ 25   (B) ₹ 35
(C) ₹ 45   (D) ₹ 50

32 If amount is ₹ 500 and interest is ₹ 100, find the principal.

(A) ₹ 100   (B) ₹ 400
(C) ₹ 600   (D) ₹ 200

33 At what rate percent per annum does a sum of ₹ 1800 become ₹ 2700 in 10 years?

(A) 5%   (B) 6%
(C) 10%   (D) 8%

34 There are 100 questions on Manu's test. She has completed 40 of the questions. What percent of the questions has Manu completed?

(A) 0.4%   (B) 4%
(C) 40%   (D) 400%

35 Raju bought a pen for ₹ 5 and sold it to Krishna for ₹ 10. What is his gain percentage?

(A) 25%   (B) 50%
(C) 100%   (D) 200%

36 The average mark of Raju in 5 tests is 70. How many marks did he get in total?

(A) 350   (B) 300
(C) 35   (D) 250

(37-40): There are 15 blue marbles and 9 red ones in a bottle.

37 What is the ratio of number of red marbles to the total number of marbles?

(A) 3 : 8   (B) 5 : 8
(C) 3 : 5   (D) 5 : 13

38 What is the ratio of number of blue marbles to the total number of marbles?

(A) 5 : 3   (B) 3 : 8
(C) 5 : 8   (D) 3 : 5

39 What percent of the marbles is blue?

(A) $62\frac{1}{2}$ %   (B) 75%
(C) $65\frac{1}{2}$ %   (D) $37\frac{1}{2}$ %

40 What is the decimal equivalent of percentage of red marbles?

(A) 0.573   (B) 0.375
(C) 0.357   (D) 0.625

41 30% of a number is 24. What is $1\frac{1}{2}$ times the number?

(A) 36   (B) 45
(C) 100   (D) 120

42 What is the difference between 25% of 50 and 250% of 20?

(A) 12.5   (B) 5
(C) 37.5   (D) 255.5

43 What is 15% of $1\frac{1}{3}$ h?

(A) 10 min   (B) 16 min
(C) 22 min   (D) 12 min

44 The average between X and Y is 108. Y is 300% the value of X. Find the difference between X and Y.

(A) 108   (B) 54
(C) 36   (D) 144

45 Of the 42 children at a party, 12 are boys and the rest are girls. Identify the simplest form of the ratio of number of girls to number of boys.

(A) 2 : 5   (B) 5 : 2
(C) 5 : 7   (D) 2 : 3

46 If ☐ : 3 has the same value as 12 : 36, what is the missing number in the box?

(A) 2   (B) 1
(C) 4   (D) 12

47 The average of 6 numbers is 12. What is the total of the 6 numbers?

(A) 60   (B) 18
(C) 72   (D) 6

(48-51): The table shows the number of pupils who borrowed books from the school library in a week.

Days	Monday	Tuesday	Wednesday	Thursday	Friday	Saturday
No. of Pupils	48	32	59	43	82	120

Study the table and answer Q. 48 to Q. 51.

48 Find the average number of pupils who borrowed books per day.

(A) 62 pupils   (B) 65 pupils
(C) 66 pupils   (D) 64 pupils

49 Find the difference between the greatest and the least number of pupils who borrowed books for the week.

(A) 88   (B) 80
(C) 60   (D) 68

50 What is the ratio of number of pupils who borrowed books on Friday and Saturday?

(A) 21 : 12   (B) 21 : 30
(C) 41 : 30   (D) 41 : 60

51 What percent of the total number of pupils borrowed books on Tuesday?

(A) $5\dfrac{3}{8}$ %   (B) $8\dfrac{1}{3}$ %

(C) $8\dfrac{1}{6}$ %   (D) $8\dfrac{2}{3}$ %

Previous Contest Questions

1 Madhu had ₹ 248. He spent 25% of it on a shirt. How much had he left?

(A) ₹ 71   (B) ₹ 203
(C) ₹ 81   (D) ₹ 186

2 Mr. Kumar earns ₹ 1000 a day. His wife earns ₹ 250 less. What is the ratio of the daily earnings of Mr. Kumar and his wife?

(A) 4 : 7   (B) 3 : 4
(C) 4 : 3   (D) 3 : 7

3 What is 20% of 3 kg 400 g?

(A) 680 g   (B) 1368 g
(C) 3 kg 420 g   (D) 2 kg 720 g

4 There are 90 pages in a book. Venu read 30% of it in one hour. How many pages of the book did he read within that hour?

(A) 33   (B) 27
(C) 36   (D) 30

5 28% of the total number of pupils in a school can swim. If the enrolment of the school is 1050, how many pupils cannot swim?

(A) 804   (B) 758
(C) 756   (D) 812

6 Observe the figure.

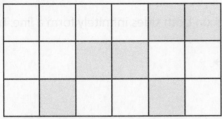

What is the ratio of the number of shaded squares to the total number of squares?

(A) 1 : 4   (B) 1 : 3
(C) 2 : 5   (D) 2 : 3

7 If P + Q = 105 and P – Q = 45, what is P : Q?

(A) 1 : 5   (B) 2 : 5
(C) 3 : 5   (D) 5 : 2

8 What is 0.1% equal to?

(A) $\dfrac{1}{10}$ (B) $\dfrac{1}{100}$

(C) $\dfrac{1}{1000}$ (D) $\dfrac{1}{10000}$

9 Srujan answered 38 out of 50 questions correctly. What percentage of the questions were answered incorrectly?

(A) 24%   (B) 12%
(C) 38%   (D) 76%

10 Observe the wooden blocks.

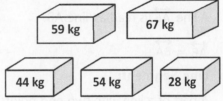

What is the average mass of the given wooden blocks?

(A) 63 kg   (B) 50.4 kg
(C) 252 kg   (D) 56.5 kg

✧ ✧ ✧

Geometry

Synopsis

◆ **Line:**

A group of points in a straight path, extending on both sides infinitely form a line. Two points on the line denote it.

A line $\overleftrightarrow{AB}$ is read as 'line AB'.

$\overleftrightarrow{AB} = \overleftrightarrow{BA}$

◆ **Line Segment:**

A part of a line with two end points is called a line segment. It has a definite length.

P •————————————• Q
Line segment

A line segment PQ is written as $\overline{PQ}$.

$\overline{PQ} = \overline{QP}$

◆ **Ray:**

A part of a line, which extends infinitely in one direction only, from a point, is a ray. The point is called the end-point of the ray.

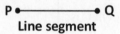

A ray OP is written as $\overrightarrow{OP}$. A ray is denoted by writing the initial point first.

So, $\overrightarrow{OP} \neq \overrightarrow{PO}$.

◆ **Angle:**

Two rays or line segments with a common end-point form an angle.

The common end-point is called the vertex of the angle and rays or line segments are called arms of the angle.

The unit of the angle is degree denoted by a small ° on the measure.

e.g., $\angle AOB = 47°$

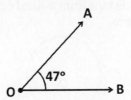

$\overrightarrow{OA}$ and $\overrightarrow{OB}$ form an angle AOB. O is the vertex of $\angle$ AOB and $\overrightarrow{OA}$ and $\overrightarrow{OB}$ are its arms or sides.

$\angle$ AOB is the same as $\angle$ BOA. Only vertex can also be used to denote an angle. Thus $\angle$ A means the angle whose vertex is A.

◆ **Types of Angles:**

(a)   An angle whose measure is between 0° and 90° is called an acute angle.

Acute angle

(b)   An angle whose measure is 90° is called a right angle.

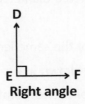

Right angle

(c)   An angle whose measure is between 90° and 180° is called obtuse angle.

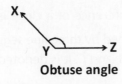

Obtuse angle

◆ **Collinear Points:** The points which lie on the same line, are called collinear points.

◆ **Non-collinear points:** The points which do not lie on the same line are called non-collinear points.

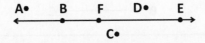

In the given figure, B, F, and E are collinear, while A, C and D are non-collinear points.

♦ **Circle:** The set of points equidistant from a fixed point is called a circle. The fixed point is called the centre of the circle.

The centre of a circle is usually denoted as O.

♦ **Radius:** The distance between the centre and any point on the circle is called the radius. All the radii of the same circle have the same length. Infinitely many radii can be drawn in a circle.

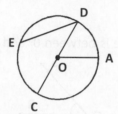

In the figure, OA = OC = OD = radius

♦ **Diameter**: A line segment that passes through the centre of the circle and whose end-points lie on the circle is called a diameter. In the figure, CD is a diameter.

Diameter = 2 × Radius

All the diameters of a circle are of the same lengths.

Infinitely many diameters can be drawn in a circle.

♦ **Chord:** A line segment which joins two points on the circumference of a circle is called a chord of the circle. A diameter is the longest chord of a circle.

♦ **Arc:** Any part of the circumference of a circle is called an arc.

♦ **Semicircle:** Half of the circumference of a circle is called a semicircle.

♦ **Triangle:** A closed figure formed by three line segments is called a triangle. A triangle is named using its vertices A, B, and C. It is denoted as △ ABC, read as triangle ABC.

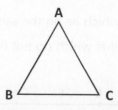

Note: △ABC can also be denoted △BCA or as △CAB.

◆ **Characteristics of a triangle:**

(a)   A triangle can be drawn only when the three given points are non-collinear.

(b)   A triangle has three vertices, three sides and three angles.

(c)   In the figure, the three line segments AB, BC and CA are the three sides of △ABC. ∠A, ∠B and ∠C are its three angles and A, B and C are its vertices.

◆ **Properties of a triangle:**

(a)   The sum of the lengths of any two sides of a triangle is greater than the length of its third side. AB + BC > AC

(b)   The difference of the lengths of any two sides of a triangle is smaller than the length of the third side. AB − BC < AC

(c)   The sum of the measures of three angles of a triangle is 180°.

(d)   In a triangle ABC, ∠ABC + ∠BAC + ∠BCA = 180°.

◆ **Quadrilateral:**

(a)   A quadrilateral is a simple closed figure bounded by four line segments.

(b)   A quadrilateral has four sides, four vertices, four angles and two diagonals (the line joining the opposite vertices.)

(c)   The sum of measures of the four angles of a quadrilateral is 360°.

◆ **Types of quadrilaterals:**

(a)   Parallelogram:

A parallelogram is a quadrilateral whose opposite sides are parallel and equal.

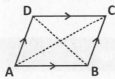

AB is parallel to DC.   AC and BD are the diagonals.

BC is parallel to AD.   AB = DC and BC = AD.

(b)   Rectangle:

A rectangle is a parallelogram in which all the angles are right angles.

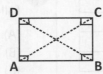

AC and BD are the diagonals. AB = DC and AD = BC. ∠A = ∠B = = ∠C = 90°

(c)   Square:

A square is a rectangle in which all sides are equal. AB = BC = CD = DA
AC and BD are the diagonals.

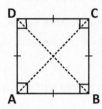

∠A = ∠B = ∠C = ∠D = 90°

(d)   Rhombus:

A rhombus is a parallelogram in which all the sides are equal.
AB = BC = CD = DA

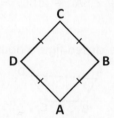

AC and BD are the diagonals.

(e) Trapezium:

A quadrilateral is called a trapezium if a pair of its opposite sides are parallel.

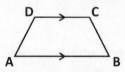

AB is parallel to DC.

Multiple Choice Questions   Ⓐ   Ⓑ   Ⓒ   Ⓓ

1   Observe the following.

	Geometrical figure	No. of end points
(P)	Line	0
(Q)	Line segment	1
(R)	Ray	2
(S)	Angle	3

Which of these is correctly matched?

(A) R   (B) Q
(C) P   (D) S

2   Find the correct match from the following.

(A) Line segment PQ = $\overrightarrow{PQ}$
(B) Line PQ = $\overleftrightarrow{PQ}$
(C) Ray PQ = $\overrightarrow{QP}$
(D) Ray QP = Ray PQ

3 Which of these is formed when two rays emerge from a common end point?

(A) A line
(B) A ray
(C) A line segment
(D) An angle

4 Which of the following is true?

(A) The common end point where two rays meet is called a ray.

(B) Angles are measured using compasses.

(C) A line segment can extend indefinitely on both sides.

(D) The common end point where two rays meet is called the vertex.

5 Name the angle which measures between 0° and 90°.

(A) An obtuse angle
(B) An acute angle
(C) A right angle
(D) A straight angle

6 Which of the following angles measures 90°?

(A) A right angle
(B) An acute angle
(C) A straight angle
(D) An obtuse angle

7 Identify the zero angle from the following.

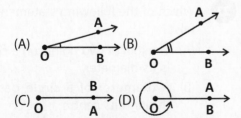

8 What is the measure of a complete angle?

(A) 2 right angles
(B) 2 straight angles
(C) 2 complete angles
(D) 4 straight angles

9 Which angle is equivalent to 4 right angles?

(A) A straight angle
(B) A reflex angle
(C) An acute angle
(D) A complete angle

10 Which instrument is used to measure or construct angles?

(A) Compasses   (B) A scale
(C) A protractor   (D) Set squares

11 How many rays can be drawn from a given point?

(A) 0   (B) 1
(C) 2   (D) Infinitely many

12 What type of an angle is formed between the hands of a clock when it is 3 O'clock?

(A) An obtuse angle
(B) A right angle
(C) A straight angle
(D) An acute angle

13 At which of these times an acute angle is formed between the hands of a clock?

(A) 5: 20 p.m.   (B) 3: 35 p.m.
(C) 9: 00 p.m.   (D) 6: 00 a.m.

14 Observe the given figure.

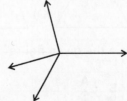

How many angles are formed in it?

(A) 4   (B) 3
(C) 2   (D) 1

15 Identify the vertex of the angle given in the figure.

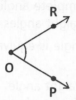

(A) R

(B) O

(C) P

(D) Both (A) and (C)

16 Observe the given angle.

Identify the arms of ∠PRQ.

(A) $\overline{RP}$

(B) $\overline{RQ}$

(C) $\overline{PR}$

(D) Both (A) and (B)

17 How many pairs of parallel lines are there in the given figure?

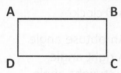

(A) 4

(B) 2

(C) 1

(D) 3

18 Identify the figure with only one pair of parallel lines.

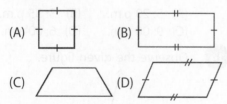

(A)

(B)

(C)

(D)

19 Observe the given figure.

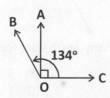

What is the measure of ∠AOB ?

(A) 44°

(B) 134°

(C) 84°

(D) 54°

20 Which of these is a set of points equidistant from a fixed point in a plane?

(A) A ray

(B) A triangle

(C) A circle

(D) A square

21 Which line segment joins the centre of a circle to a point on it?

(A) A diameter

(B) A radius

(C) A chord

(D) An

22 Which of these is a line segment joining any two points on a circle?

(A) A chord

(B) An arc

(C) A semicircle

(D) A ray

23 Which instrument is used to draw a circle?

(A) A ruler

(B) Compasses

(C) Set squares

(D) A protractor

24 Which is the longest chord of a circle?

(A) A radius

(B) An arc

(C) A diameter

(D) A semicircle

25 What is the perimeter of a circle named as?

(A) A diameter

(B) A semicircle

(C) A radius

(D) Circumference

26 Find the radius of a circle of diameter 9.2 cm.

(A) 4.6 cm

(B) 9.2 cm

(C) 4.1 cm

(D) 13.8 cm

27 Which of the following statements is false?

(A) The join of two points on a circle is its diameter.

(B) A diameter of a circle passes through its centre.

(C) A semicircle is an arc.

(D) The length of a circle is called its circumference.

28 How many radii can be drawn in a circle?

(A) 1   (B) About 10
(C) Over 100   (D) Infinitely many

29 How many semicircles can be drawn in a circle?

(A) 1   (B) 3
(C) 2   (D) Infinitely many

30 Which of these is true?

(A) A simple closed figure bounded by five line segments is called a square.

(B) A simple closed figure bounded by three line segments is called a triangle.

(C) An angle is formed by three rays with a common end point.

(D) A square has only one pair of parallel line segments.

31 Study the given sentences.

(i)	A set of points which lie on the same line are called collinear points.
(ii)	A set of points at different distances from a fixed point is a circle.
(iii)	A set of points which do not lie on the same line are called non-collinear points.

Which of the following is true?

(A) Only (i)
(B) Only (ii)
(C) Only (i) and (ii)
(D) Only (i) and (iii)

32 Study the table given.

	Figure	No. of Vertices
(i)	Square	4
(ii)	Triangle	3
(iii)	Circle	5
(iv)	Rectangle	6

Which of the following is correct?

(A) Only (i) and (ii)
(B) Only (ii) and (iii)
(C) Only (iii) and (iv)
(D) Only (i) and (iv)

33 Find the sum of the three angles in a triangle.

(A) 3 right angles (B) 4 right angles
(C) 2 right angles (D) 270°

34 Study the following.

X: The sum of the lengths of two sides of a triangle.

Y: The third side of the same triangle.

Which relation is true?

(A) X = Y   (B) X > Y
(C) X < Y   (D) Either (A) and (C)

35 The lengths of two sides of a triangle are 4 cm and 7 cm. Which of the following can be the measure of its third side?

(A) 13 cm   (B) 12 cm
(C) 11 cm   (D) 3 cm

36 Observe the figure given.

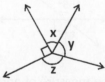

What is the measure of x + y + z?

(A) 90°   (B) 270°
(C) 360°   (D) 180°

37 How many more of the basic shape shown are needed to fill the box up?

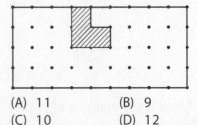

(A) 11   (B) 9
(C) 10   (D) 12

38 What is the unit shape used for the given tessellation?

(A) 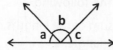   (B)

(C)   (D)

39 Observe the given figure.

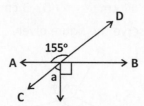

If ∠b = 62° and ∠c = 77°, find ∠a.

(A) 39°   (B) 141°
(C) 41°   (D) 139°

40 What is $\frac{5}{6}$ of a complete turn equal to?

(A) 180°   (B) 360°
(C) 90°   (D) 300°

41 Study the figure given.

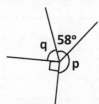

Find the measure of angle 'a'.

(A) 65°   (B) 90°
(C) 35°   (D) 25°

42 In the figure, ∠p is three times the size of ∠q.

What is the measure of ∠p?

(A) 53°   (B) 148°
(C) 159°   (D) 212°

43 In the given figure, if ∠x = ∠y = ∠z, find the sum of ∠w and ∠x.

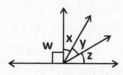

(A) 120°   (B) 60°
(C) 90°   (D) 180°

44 The figure shows a circle with centre O.

Identify the chord that is a diameter.

(A) PN   (B) PQ
(C) NQ   (D) MN

45 What is the measure of the given angle?

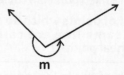

(A) 270°   (B) 180°
(C) 90°   (D) 250°

46 Which of the following shapes cannot be tessellated?

(A)   (B)

(C)   (D)

47 Lines AB and CD intersect at O.

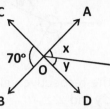

Given ∠x : ∠y = 3 : 2, find ∠x.

(A) 70°   (B) 42°
(C) 140°   (D) 81°

48 PQ and RS are two straight lines meeting at O.

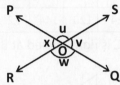

Which of the following statements is false?

(A) ∠u = ∠w
(B) ∠x = ∠v
(C) ∠x = ∠v = 180°
(D) ∠x = ∠u = 180°

49 In the figure, ∠x is 36° less than ∠y.

Find the measure of ∠y.

(A) 179°   (B) 96°
(C) 134°   (D) 143°

50 In the given figure, AB, CD and EF are straight lines.

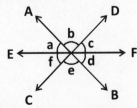

Given ∠a = 43°, find ∠e + ∠f.

(A) 137°   (B) 101°
(C) 122°   (D) 79°

Previous Contest Questions

1 The present time is 4 o'clock.

Through how many degrees will the hour hand move in 10 hours?

(A) 360°   (B) 300°
(C) 340°   (D) 345°

2 In the given figure, ∠x is $\frac{2}{3}$ of ∠y. AB, PQ and CD are straight lines.

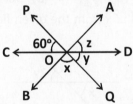

What is ∠x expressed as a fraction of ∠z?

(A) $\frac{1}{3}$ (B) $\frac{1}{2}$

(C) $\frac{2}{3}$ (D) $\frac{3}{4}$

3 In the following figure, WX and YZ are straight lines.

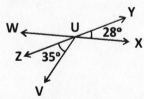

Find ∠WUZ.

(A) ∠ZUV   (B) ∠YUX
(C) ∠WUY   (D) ∠XUV

4 AD and BE are straight lines.

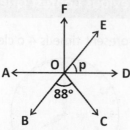

Given that ∠AOB = ∠DOC, find ∠p.

(A) 44°   (B) 46°
(C) 51°   (D) 92°

5 Find the value of x°.

(A) 15°   (B) 30°
(C) 18°   (D) 36°

6 Find ∠x from the given figure.

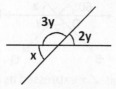

(A) 36°   (B) 62°
(C) 72°   (D) 108°

7 In the figure, ∠w, ∠x, ∠y and ∠z are in the ratio 1 : 3 : 5 : 6.

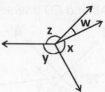

Find the respective values of ∠w, ∠x, ∠y and ∠z.

	∠w	∠x	∠y	∠z
(A)	24°	72°	120°	144°
(B)	24°	72°	144°	120°
(C)	24°	120°	72°	144°
(D)	24°	120°	144°	72°

8 Δ ABC is right angled at B.

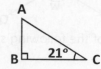

Find ∠BAC.

(A) 59°   (B) 69°
(C) 79°   (D) 89°

9 PQRS is a trapezium.

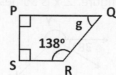

Find ∠g.

(A) 42°   (B) 48°
(C) 62°   (D) 69°

◇ ◇ ◇

Mensuration

◆ **Perimeter :**

The total boundary length of a closed figure is called its perimeter. It is expressed in usual units of measurement of length.

◆ **Area :**

The amount of surface enclosed by a closed figure is called its area.

(a) Area is measured in square units.

(b) 1 m = 100 cm ; 1 sq m = 10000 sq cm;

(c) 1 cm = 10 mm ; 1 sq cm = 100 sq mm

◆ **Volume :**

The space occupied by an object is called its volume.

(a) Volume is measured in cubic units.

(b) 1 cu m = 1000000 cu cm;

(c) 1 cu cm = 1000 cu mm

◆ **Cube :**

It is a solid figure with 6 square surfaces.

◆ Volume of a cube = edge × edge × edge cu units.

◆ **Cuboid :**

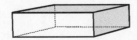

It is a solid figure with 6 rectangular surfaces.

◆   Volume of a cuboid = length × breadth × height cubic units.

$V = l \times b \times h$

$$\therefore \quad l = \frac{V}{bh}; \qquad\qquad b = \frac{V}{lh}; \qquad\qquad h = \frac{V}{lb}$$

◆   The shape obtained on opening a solid shape is called a net.

◆   A net can be folded back or closed into form a solid.

◆   **Net of a cube :**

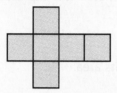

The net of a cube has 6 squares.

◆   **Net of a cuboid :**

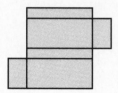

The net of a cuboid has 6 rectangles.

Multiple Choice Questions

1 What is the sum of the sides of a triangle?

(A) The length of its sides
(B) Its area
(C) Its perimeter
(D) All the above

2 Find the missing number.

> The perimeter of a square is the sum of the lengths of its _____ sides.

(A) 3   (B) 2
(C) 5   (D) 4

3 What is the perimeter of the given figure if all the measures are in cm?

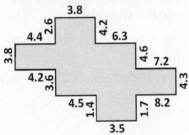

(A) 68.2 cm   (B) 68.1 cm
(C) 86.3 cm   (D) 68.3 cm

4 What is the perimeter of a rectangle whose length(l) and breadth (b) are given?

(A) $2(l \times b)$ units (B) $(2l + 2b)$ units
(C) $2l + 3b$ units (D) $l \times b$ units

5 Which of the following gives the area of a square?

(A) side × side   (B) 3 × side
(C) side × 4   (D) $l \times b$

6 Which among the following gives the area of a rectangle?

(A) length × 4
(B) length × breadth
(C) 3 × length
(D) breadth × 6

7 Find the area of a square whose side measures 13 m.

(A) 9 m   (B) 9 sq m
(C) 169 sq m   (D) 169 m

8 What is the area of a rectangle of length 13 m and breadth 12 m?

(A) 156 m   (B) 156 cm
(C) 156 sq m   (D) 156 sq cm

9 If the length and breadth of a rectangle are doubled how does its perimeter change?

(A) Tripled
(B) Doubled
(C) Halved
(D) Remains the same

10 The area of a rectangle is 120 sq m and its breadth is 5 m. Find its length.

(A) 204 m   (B) 24 m
(C) 28 m   (D) 26 m

11 The area of square is 144 sq m. What is the measure of its side?

(A) 13 m   (B) 14 m
(C) 12 m   (D) 11 m

12 The length of a rectangular hall is 32 m. If it can be partitioned into two equal square rooms, what is the length of the partition?

(A) 16 m   (B) 8 m
(C) 4 m   (D) 32 m

13 The length of a rectangle is $\frac{6}{5}$ of its breadth. If its perimeter is 132 m, find its area.

(A) 1080 m²   (B) 640 m²
(C) 1620 m²   (D) 2160 m²

14 The side of a square tile is 10 cm. How many tiles can be fixed on one side of a wall which is 2.5 m long and 2 m high?

(A) 100   (B) 400
(C) 5000   (D) 500

15 What is the amount of surface enclosed by a closed plane figure?

(A) Area   (B) Perimeter
(C) Volume   (D) Circumference

16 Find the volume of a cube of edge 25 cm.

(A) 16525 cu cm   (B) 15652 cu cm
(C) 15625 cu cm   (D) 15620 cu cm

17 Find the volume of a cuboid of dimensions 10 cm, 12 cm and 8 cm.

(A) 96 cc   (B) 9.6 cc
(C) 960 cu m   (D) 960 cu cm

18 Identify the solid figure with 6 square surfaces.

(A) A cuboid   (B) A rectangle
(C) A square   (D) A cube

19 Find the volume of a cube whose edge is $\frac{1}{4}$ cm.

(A) $\frac{1}{16}$ cu cm   (B) $\frac{1}{32}$ cu cm

(C) $\frac{1}{64}$ cu cm   (D) $\frac{1}{28}$ cu cm

20 The edge of a cube is 25 m. The dimensions of a cuboid are l = 20m, b = 2 m, h = 3 m. Which of the following is correct?

(A) The volume of the cube is greater than that of the cuboid.

(B) The volume of the cuboid is greater than that of the cube.

(C) Both the cube and the cuboid have the same volume.

(D) Either (A) or (C).

21 Study the following.

> P : The volume of a cube of side 12 m.
>
> Q : The volume of a cuboid of dimensions 8 m × 6 m × 4m.

Which of the following is correct?

(A) P > Q   (B) P < Q
(C) P = Q   (D) P = 4Q

22 Find the capacity of a box that measures 9 cm × 3.5 cm × 7.5 cm.

(A) 236.25 cm³   (B) 189 cm³
(C) 236.25 m³   (D) 189 m³

23 A cuboid measuring 10 cm by 2.5 cm by 5 cm has the same volume as a cube. What is the measure of the edge of the cube?

(A) 125 cm   (B) 15 cm
(C) 10 cm   (D) 5 cm

24 The shaded area of the two faces of a cube is 72 m².

What is the volume of the cube?

(A) 216 m³   (B) 625 m³
(C) 64 m³   (D) 265 m³

25 How many cubes must be added to solid A so that it becomes solid B?

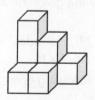

Solid A   Solid B

(A) 8   (B) 19
(C) 11   (D) 27

26 A cube of edge 9 cm was filled with 405 cm³ of water. What is the height of water in the cube?

(A) 9 cm   (B) 81 cm
(C) 5 cm   (D) 25 cm

27 What fraction of the volume of the cube is the volume of the cuboid?

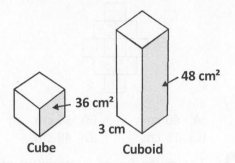

Cube   Cuboid

(A) $\dfrac{1}{3}$ (B) $\dfrac{2}{3}$

(C) $\dfrac{1}{4}$ (D) $\dfrac{2}{5}$

28 A rectangular tank 15 cm long, 12 cm wide and 8 cm high was completely filled with water. Find the volume of water in the tank.

(A) 180 cm³   (B) 440 cm³
(C) 1200 cm³   (D) 1440 cm³

29 A rectangular tank measuring 20 cm by 30 cm by 45 cm is filled with water to its brim. Find the capacity of the tank.

(A) 27 l
(B) 27000 cm³
(C) Both (A) and (B)
(D) Neither (A) nor (B)

30 The area of a carpet is 12 m². If its length is 8 m, what is its breadth?

(A) 1.5 m   (B) 2.8 m
(C) 1.2 m   (D) 0.96 m

31 What is the perimeter of a square tile whose area is 64 cm²?

(A) 64 cm   (B) 16 cm
(C) 8 cm   (D) 32 cm

32 A piece of wire is bent to form a square of area 49 cm². What is the length of the piece of wire?

(A) 28 cm   (B) 28 cm²
(C) 28 m²   (D) 28 m

33 A tank has 2250 cm³ of water. 6430 cm³ of water is poured into the tank to fill it to the full. What is the capacity of the tank?

(A) 868 l (B) 86.8 l
(C) 8.68 l (D) 8680 l

34 Find the total volume of 4 exactly similar cubes of side 5 cm.

(A) 125 cm³   (B) 100 cm³
(C) 600 cm³   (D) 500 cm³

(35-37): The net given is of an open top cube. Each side of the square in the net is 4 cm long.

4 cm
4 cm

35 What is the perimeter of the given net?

(A) 32 cm   (B) 64 cm
(C) 24 cm   (D) 48 cm

36 What is the area of the cardboard needed to make the given net?

(A) 80 cm²   (B) 20 cm²
(C) 16 cm²   (D) 100 cm²

37 What is the capacity of the cube that can be made using the given net?

(A) 16 cm³   (B) 64 cm³
(C) 164 cm³   (D) 36 cm³

38 Which one of the following has the greatest volume?

(A) A fish tank of capacity 965 cm³.

(B) A 1.25 l bottle of water.

(C) A cube of side 9 cm.

(D) A box measuring 5 cm by 2 cm by 1 cm.

39 A 2-litre bottle is half-filled with water. How much more water must be added to fill up the bottle completely?

(A) $\frac{1}{2}$ cm³ (B) 100 cm³

(C) 500 cm³ (D) 1000 cm³

40 Observe the given solid.

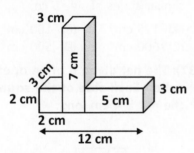

Find its volume.

(A) 48 cm³ (B) 68 cm³

(C) 72 cm³ (D) 162 cm³

(41-42): Observe the given figures.

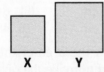

The perimeter of square X is 20 cm, and that of square Y is 36 cm.

41 What is the difference in the length of each side of the squares?

(A) 4 cm (B) 5 cm

(C) 14 cm (D) 9 cm

42 What is their total area?

(A) 25 cm² (B) 106 cm²

(C) 56 cm² (D) 81 cm²

43 Find the perimeter of the given figure, if it is made up of identical squares of sides 3 cm.

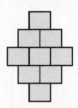

(A) 60 cm (B) 36 cm

(C) 16 cm (D) 48 cm

44 The given figure is made up of a triangle and a square of area 144 cm².

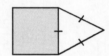

What is the perimeter of the figure?

(A) 72 cm (B) 60 cm

(C) 360 cm (D) 12 cm

45 In the given figure, each of the two equal sides of triangle PQR is 1.5 times the length of PQ.

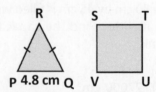

The ratio of the perimeter of square STUV to that of △ PQR is 4 : 3. What is the area of the square?

(A) 23.04 m² (B) 25.6 m²

(C) 40.96 m² (D) 655.36 m²

Previous Contest Questions

1 The length of a rectangle is 8 times its breadth. If the perimeter of the rectangle is 61.2 m, find the difference between the length and the breadth of the rectangle.

(A) 238 cm   (B) 2380 cm
(C) 23.8 cm   (D) 2830 cm

2 What is the total volume of the smallest number of cubes that must be added to make the given figure a cuboid?

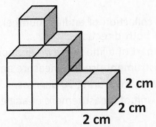

2 cm
2 cm
2 cm

(A) 104 cm³   (B) 64 cm³
(C) 27 cm³   (D) 13 cm³

3 The height of the water level in a tank is 5 cm. It contains 625 cm³ of water. Find its base area.

(A) 81 cm²   (B) 625 cm²
(C) 125 cm²   (D) 50 cm²

4 The ratio of the perimeter of a rectangle to its length is 10 : 3. If its breadth is 8 cm, what is the area of the rectangle?

(A) 81 cm²   (B) 64 cm²
(C) 25 cm²   (D) 96 cm²

5 The perimeter of rectangle PQRS is 28 cm.

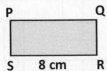

P   Q

S   8 cm   R

What is the ratio of its length to its breadth?

(A) 3 : 4   (B) 4 : 3
(C) 4 : 5   (D) 3 : 7

6 The ratio of the length of a rectangle to its breadth is 5 : 2. If its area is 1690 cm², find the perimeter of the rectangle.

(A) 182 cm   (B) 169 cm
(C) 196 cm   (D) 264 cm

7 A container 12 cm deep is 10 cm wide and 17 cm long. It is half-filled with rice. How many cubic centimetres of rice is there in the container?

(A) 1020 cm³   (B) 2040 cm³
(C) 510 cm³   (D) 4080 cm³

8 The given cuboid is made up of 3 cm cubes.

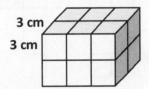

3 cm
3 cm

What is its volume?

(A) 27 cm³   (B) 108 cm³
(C) 162 cm³   (D) 324 cm³

9 In the given figure, the rectangle has the same perimeter as the square.

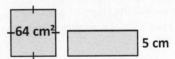

64 cm²   5 cm

If the breadth of the rectangle is 5 cm, what is its area?

(A) 55 cm³   (B) 55 m²
(C) 55 cm²   (D) 55 km²

10 The sides of a triangle are in the ratio 3 : 4 : 5. If the longest side is 15 cm, what is the perimeter of the triangle?

(A) 18 cm   (B) 48 cm
(C) 24 cm   (D) 36 cm

CROSSWORD

6. Geometry

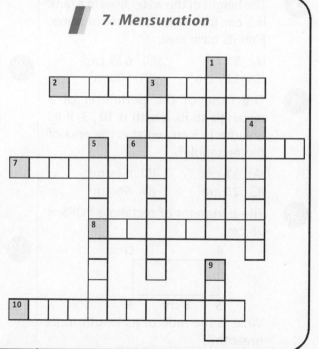

ACROSS

2 Two lines meeting at a point.
7 The middle letter in the name of an angle.
8 An angle measuring 180 degrees.
9 Angle less than a right angle.
10 A part of a line that has one endpoint, extending only in one direction.

DOWN

1 A collection of endless number of points in both directions.
3 A part of a line with two endpoints.
4 Instrument used to measure an angle.
5 Angle measuring 90 degrees.
6 A unit of measurement of angles.

7. Mensuration

ACROSS

2 Units for measuring area.
6 The areas of figures with same perimeter.
7 The figure whose perimeter is four times its side.
8 The sum of the edges of a figure.
10 Units of area of the black board in your class.

DOWN

1 The perimeters of figures with same area.
3 The method used for finding the area of irregular shapes.
4 If P is the perimeter and l the length of a rectangle, this is given as $\dfrac{p}{2} - l$.
5 This is useful for finding the area of irregular shapes.
9 The amount of surface covered by a figure.

Measurement

- **Basic units:**

    Length - metre (m)   Mass (Weight) - gram (g)   Capacity (Volume)- litre (l)

    Time - second (s)   Temperature - degree celsius (°C)

- Lengths are measured using millimetres (mm), centimetres (cm) metres (m) and kilometres (km).

    1 cm = 10 mm;   1 m = 100 cm;   1 km = 1000 m

- Mass or weight of an object is measured using milligrams (mg), grams (g) and kilograms (kg).

    1 g = 1000 mg; 1 kg = 1000 g;   1 tonne = 1000 kg

- Capacity is measured using millilitres (ml), litres (l) and kilolitres (kl).

    1 l = 1000 ml; 1 kl = 1000 l

- Time is measured in seconds (s), minutes (min), hours (h). Larger durations are measured in days, weeks, months, years, decades, centuries etc.,

    1 hour = 60 minutes;   1 minute = 60 seconds

- To convert a bigger unit to a smaller unit, multiply by the conversion factor.

- To convert a smaller unit to a bigger unit, divide by the conversion factor.

- **Conversions:**

    a) Length:

    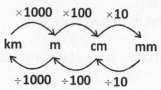

    b) Mass:

    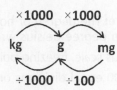

    c) Capacity:

    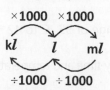

    d) Time:

    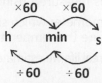

    To express length, mass or capacity using bigger unit, we use decimals.

- **Duration of time:** The time spent during an event or activity is called the duration of time, or elapsed time.

a) To find the finishing time, add the elapsed time to the starting time.

Finishing time = Starting time + Elapsed time

> **Note:** We count forward to find the finishing time.

b) To find the starting time, subtract the elapsed time from the finishing time.

Starting time = Finishing time – Elapsed time

> **Note:** We count backwards from the finishing time to find the starting time.

◆ To find the finishing date, add the duration to the starting date.

Finishing date = Duration + Starting date

> **Note:** We count forward to find the finishing date.

Starting date = Finishing date – Duration

> **Note:** We count backward to find the starting date.

1 century = 100 years = 10 decades

1 decade = 10 years

1 year = 12 months;   1 month = $\frac{1}{12}$ year

1 week = 7 days;   1 day = $\frac{1}{7}$ week

1 day = 24 hours;   1 hour = $\frac{1}{24}$ day

1 hour = 60 minutes;   1 minute = $\frac{1}{60}$ hour

1 minute = 60 seconds;   1 second = $\frac{1}{60}$ minute

◆ **Temperature:** The degree of hotness of a body is called its temperature. It is measured in degree Celsius written as °C.

On the Celsius scale, freezing point of water is 0 °C and boiling point of water is 100 °C

There are 100 equal divisions on the Celsius scale.

The temperature of a normal human being is 37 °C.

Temperature is measured using a thermometer.

◆ A clinical thermometer which shows the temperature in the range of 35 °C to 42 °C is used to measure the temperature of a human body.

◆ **Estimation:** In real life we estimate measures of length, mass, capacity, time and temperature.

Multiple Choice Questions      A B C D

1 Study the following.

526.8 kg – 287.93 kg = P kg Q g

What are the respective values of P and Q?

(A) 238, 87   (B) 237, 88
(C) 814, 73   (D) 87, 238

2 Bhavani's present age is 11 years 3 months. How old will she be in 18 months' time?

(A) 13 years 3 months
(B) 11 years 9 months
(C) 12 years 9 months
(D) 12 years 6 months

3 A piece of string was cut into 12 equal pieces. The length of 5 such pieces is $\frac{15}{8}$ m. Find the length of the original piece of string.

(A) 4.8 cm   (B) 4.5 cm
(C) 0.375 cm   (D) 4.5 m

4 What is the boiling point of water on the celsius scale?

(A) 10 °C   (B) 100 °C
(C) 50 °C   (D) 37 °C

5 What fraction of 73 l 80 ml is 3.6 l?

(A) $\frac{2}{41}$ (B) $\frac{1}{203}$

(C) $\frac{10}{203}$ (D) $\frac{10}{23}$

6 Which of the following is the ratio of 1 m 5 cm to 3.5 km?

(A) 3 : 7   (B) 3 : 10
(C) 3 : 700   (D) 3 : 10000

7 A tailor can alter 8 shirts in 39 minutes. At this rate, how many shirts can he alter in $3\frac{1}{4}$ hours?

(A) 32   (B) 40
(C) 45   (D) 36

8 Roja bought $1\frac{1}{2}$ kg of sugar. Kamala bought half as much sugar as Roja. What was the total mass of sugar bought by both of them?

(A) $2\frac{1}{4}$ kg   (B) $2\frac{1}{2}$ kg

(C) $4\frac{1}{2}$ kg   (D) 3 kg

9 43.16 l of juice was transferred into a barrel containing 39 l 30 ml of juice. What is the total volume of juice in the barrel?

(A) 81 l 790 ml (B) 83 l 350 l
(C) 85 l 60 ml (D) 82 l 190 ml

10 Observe the line given.

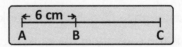

If the ratio of the length of AB to the length of BC is 2 : 5, find the length of AC.

(A) 21 cm   (B) 15 cm
(C) 30 cm   (D) 9 cm

11 Girish can paint 9 flowers in 3 minutes. At this rate, how many flowers can he paint in 120 seconds?

(A) 18   (B) 27
(C) 12   (D) 6

12 5 l of syrup was poured into bottles of 300 ml each. How much more syrup was needed to completely fill all the bottles used?

(A) 150 ml (B) 100 ml
(C) 250 ml (D) 200 ml

13 What is the temperature at which water freezes?

(A) 0 °C   (B) 36.5 °C
(C) 37 °C   (D) 100 °C

14 A box full of buttons has a mass of 2 kg. When it is $\frac{1}{3}$ full, its mass is only 800 g. What is the mass of the box?

(A) 200 g   (B) 150 g
(C) 1200 g   (D) 600 g

15 How many equal divisions are there on the Celsius scale?

(A) 1000   (B) 50
(C) 100   (D) 200

16 A typist can type 2520 words in 1 hour. How long will she take to type 1680 words?

(A) 28 minutes   (B) 40 minutes
(C) 42 minutes   (D) 840 minutes

17 A container has 16 l of water. This is enough to fill only $\frac{1}{4}$ of a tank. What is the capacity of the tank?

(A) 48 l (B) 40 l
(C) 64 l (D) 72 l

18 Rajesh left the office 1 h 25 min before noon. What time did Rajesh leave the office?

(A) 10: 35 a.m.   (B) 11: 35 a.m.
(C) 01: 25 p.m.   (D) 10: 35 p.m.

19 The ratio of Anita's mass to Mamata's mass is 4 : 7. If their total mass is 99 kg, what is Mamata's mass?

(A) 63 kg   (B) 45 kg
(C) 36 kg   (D) 54 kg

20 Praveen bought 5 tins of orange juice each containing 0.75 l of orange juice. He poured the orange juice into a 6-litre container. How many more tins must Praveen buy to fill up the container with orange juice?

(A) 30   (B) 2
(C) 5   (D) 3

21 The normal body temperature of some warm-blooded creatures is given in the table.

Creature	Temperature
Bat	28 °C
Man	37 °C
Bird	40 °C
Spiny ant eater	30 °C

The temperature of which creature when rounded to the nearest ten is 30 °C?

(A) Bat   (B) Man
(C) Bird   (D) Spiny ant eater

22 65 ml of orange juice is mixed with 0.835 l of water in a container. The mixture is then poured into cups of 0.09 l each. How many cups are needed?

(A) 1000   (B) 1000
(C) 1   (D) 10

23 27th February 2013 was a Wednesday. What day was 27th March, the same year?

(A) Sunday   (B) Wednesday
(C) Monday   (D) Friday

24 Sudhir has a mass of 25 kg. His mother is twice as heavy as Sudhir. Sudhir's brother has a mass of $\frac{1}{4}$ of his mother's mass. What is the mass of Sudhir's brother?

(A) 13 kg 500 g   (B) 12 kg
(C) 12 kg 500 g   (D) 13 kg

25 A 35.08 cm long wire is cut into 2 pieces. One piece is bent into a square of side 2.8 cm. What is the length of the other piece?

(A) 23 cm   (B) 24.88 cm
(C) 24 cm   (D) 23.88 cm

26 Observe the given thermometer.

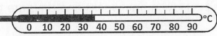

Which temperature of human beings does the thermometer show?

(A) High fever
(B) Low fever
(C) Normal body temperature
(D) Very high fever

27 A video recorder is four times as heavy as a camera. What is the mass of the camera if the mass of a video recorder is 2400 g?

(A) 600 kg   (B) 6 kg
(C) 6000 kg   (D) 0.6 kg

28 The parking fee at a certain car park is ₹ 12.50 per hour or part thereof. How much must one pay for parking his car there for $5\frac{1}{2}$ hours?

(A) ₹ 68.75   (B) ₹ 6.25
(C) ₹ 60.50   (D) ₹ 30.75

29 Smriti used 40% of a piece of 6-m long cloth to make 4 flags and the remainder to make some skirts. If each skirt required 1.2 m of cloth, how many skirts did she make?

(A) 13   (B) 30
(C) 4   (D) 3

30 A machine can produce 720 toys in 8 minutes. How many toys can it produce in 6 minutes?

(A) 1440   (B) 240
(C) 540   (D) 320

31 Containers A and B had 15 *l* and 5 *l* of water respectively. When an equal amount of water was poured into both containers, container A had twice the volume of water as container B. What was the least amount of water that was poured into each container?

(A) 5 m*l*   (B) 5000 m*l*
(C) 50 m*l*   (D) 500 m*l*

32 24 cups of water are needed to fill $\frac{3}{5}$ of a basin. How many cups are needed to fill $\frac{1}{2}$ of the basin?

(A) 15   (B) 35
(C) 20   (D) 40

33 The total length of a rope, a string and a chain is 132.2 m. The rope is 1210 cm longer than the string. The chain is 4 times as long as the rope. How much longer is the chain than the string?

(A) 24.05 m   (B) 84.25 m
(C) 96.2 m   (D) 11.95 m

34 On a certain day, the temperatures recorded at different times is as shown in the table.

Time	Temperature
8: 00 a.m.	24 °C
12: 00 noon	36 °C
4: 00 p.m.	34 °C
8: 00 p.m.	30 °C

Between which times is the increase in temperature the maximum?

(A) 8: 00 a.m. – 12: 00 noon
(B) 12 noon – 8: 00 p.m.
(C) 12 noon – 4: 00 p.m.
(D) 4: 00 p.m. – 8: 00 p.m.

35 7 similar iron balls and 4 similar steel balls have a total mass of 7.4 kg. Find the mass of each steel ball if each iron ball weighs 560 g.

(A) 870 g   (B) 3480 g
(C) 780 g   (D) 3920 g

36 Observe the given beakers.

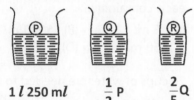

1 l 250 ml $\frac{1}{2}$ P $\frac{2}{5}$ Q

What is the volume of the liquid in beaker R?

(A) 250 ml (B) 216 ml
(C) 271 ml (D) 261 ml

37 Water flows into a tank at a rate of 350 ml per minute. How much water will be there in the tank after $\frac{3}{4}$ hour?

(A) 15.075 l (B) 1575 l
(C) 15.75 l (D) 15750 l

38 20 kg of cashew nuts are divided into two boxes in the ratio 2 : 3. How many grams of cashew nuts are there in the lighter box?

(A) 1200 g   (B) 8000 g
(C) 800 g   (D) 12000 g

39 What date is it 19 days before 30th April?

(A) 11th April   (B) 19th May
(C) 19th April   (D) 11th May

40 Sharat bought 3 l of orange juice. He drank 0.196 l on Monday and 200 ml on Tuesday. He stored the rest equally in 30 bottles. How much juice was there in each bottle?

(A) 86.8 ml (B) 88.6 ml
(C) 86.6 ml (D) 68.8 ml

41 Some flag poles were placed at equal distances 2 m apart along the perimeter of a rectangular field. The field measures 38 m by 24 m. How many flag poles were there around the field?

(A) 64   (B) 62
(C) 58   (D) 60

42 How many weeks and days are there in 1440 days?

(A) 25 weeks 30 days
(B) 250 weeks 3 days
(C) 25 weeks 5 days
(D) 205 weeks 5 days

43 Which of the following is incorrect?

(A) 3 kg 20 g = 3.02 kg
(B) 5 kg 5 g = 5.005 kg
(C) 230 g = 0.23 kg
(D) 8 kg 80 g = 8.008 kg

44 Observe the categorisation of days based on the recorded temperatures.

Temperature	Day
20 °C – 25 °C	Mild weather
25 °C – 30 °C	Warm weather
0 °C – 10 °C	Cold weather
30 °C – 35 °C	Hot weather

Mr. Varma's family planned to go on a picnic. What is the range of temperature suitable to go on a picnic?

(A) 0° - 10 °C   (B) 20 °C - 25 °C
(C) 30 °C - 35 °C   (D) 25 °C - 30 °C

45 A shopkeeper had 600 kg of sugar. He sold 252 kg. What percentage of sugar is remaining?

(A) 48%   (B) 62%
(C) 58%   (D) 42%

 Previous Contest Questions

1 Shruti had $\frac{5}{6}$ kg of butter. She used $\frac{1}{3}$ kg of it to bake some biscuits and $\frac{1}{12}$ kg to bake a cake. How much butter is remaining with her (approximately)?

(A) 417 g   (B) 500 g
(C) 420 g   (D) 415 g

2 The mid-day temperature on a Sunday was 34 °C. If fell by 9 °C by 8: 00 p.m. on Sunday and further by 3 °C by 2: 00 a.m. the next day. The temperature rose by 8 °C by 8: 00 a.m. on Monday. What is the temperature at 8: 00 a.m. on Monday?

(A) 12 °C   (B) 30 °C
(D) 46 °C   (D) 22 °C

3 Sunitha is 65 years old and her son is 36 years old. How many years ago was sunitha's age twice the age of her son?

(A) 8   (B) 6
(C) 12   (D) 7

4 Observe the given figure in which the heights of two poles P and Q are given.

If the height of pole P is 225 cm, how much shorter than 3 m is pole Q?

(A) 180 cm   (B) 120 cm
(C) 140 cm   (D) 160 cm

5 An iron rod, heated to 120 °C is kept in the open. The rod loses 2 °C temperature every minute. What would the temperature of the rod be after 16 minutes?

(A) 88 °C   (B) 98 °C
(C) 78 °C   (D) 32 °C

6 Satish bought $14\frac{2}{3}$ kg of flour and his friend bought $10\frac{1}{4}$ kg of flour. Together, they used $20\frac{5}{6}$ kg of flour to make some rotis. How much flour was remaining with them?

(A) $4\frac{1}{4}$ kg   (B) $3\frac{1}{4}$ kg

(C) $4\frac{11}{12}$ kg   (D) $4\frac{1}{12}$ kg

7 Amruta started painting a picture at 10 a.m. She stopped for lunch at 12: 30 p.m. and resumed painting an hour later. How long did she actually spend painting if she finished at 2 p.m.?

(A) $4\frac{1}{2}$ h   (B) 4 h

(C) 3 h   (D) $3\frac{1}{2}$ h

8 The heights of some children are given in the box.

Name	Height
Mahesh	78 cm
John	90 cm
Bhaskar	?
Average	84 cm

What is the height of Bhaskar?

(A) 168 cm   (B) 84 cm
(C) 78 cm   (D) 90 cm

9 Water in a vessel is at a temperature of 38.5 °C. By how much must its temperature be increased so as to boil it?

(A) 38.5 °C   (B) 100 °C
(C) 61.5 °C   (D) 82.5 °C

(10-11): Water from a faulty tap drips at the rate of 250 ml per minute.

10 How much water can be collected in 12 minutes?

(A) 3 l (B) 2.875 l
(C) 2.5 l (D) 3.500 l

11 How long will it take to fill a container of capacity 8 l from the dripping tap?

(A) 40 min   (B) 16 min
(C) 30 min   (D) 32 min

12 The mass of a basket of fruits is 17000 g corrected to the nearest thousand grams. What could be the greatest mass of the basket of fruits?

(A) 16500 g   (B) 16499 g
(C) 17499 g   (D) 17500 g

CHAPTER 9

Data Handling

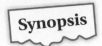
Synopsis

◆ **Data :**

   (a) Collection of information in numerical form for a specific purpose is called data.

   (b) Data can be analysed and inferences are drawn from them.

   (c) The numerical data are represented in pictorial form for easy analysis and interpretation.

◆ **Data presentation:**

   (a) Data are usually presented in the form of tables (numerical form) and pictures and graphs (pictorial representation).

   (b) Representation of data using pictures is called pictograph.

   (c) It is very tedious and time consuming to draw pictures for large data.

   (d) Bar graphs can be drawn to represent data using rectangles or bars.

   (e) In a bar graph, bars of equal width and heights corresponding to the given data are drawn.

   (f) The number of bars in a bar graph is the same as the number of values in the given data.

   (g) The spaces between the bars should have the same width.

   (h) A bar graph should be given a title at the top or bottom of the graph.

   (i) Scale should be mentioned in the upper part of the graph.

◆ **Circle graphs or pie-charts:** A full circle represents a whole, 1 or 100%, semicircle half, $\frac{1}{2}$ or 50% and a quarter circle a fourth, $\frac{1}{4}$ or 25%.

   (a) A pie-chart is used for comparison.

   (b) The various parts in a pie-chart are represented as a percentage, a fraction or a decimal.

   (c) A tally chart is drawn by drawing the no. of lines for each value in the data.

> *Note:* 4 lines (vertical) are drawn side by side to denote 4 (IIII). 5 is denoted by crossing the four vertical lines (IIII).

   (d) A line graph can be drawn by joining the dots for the values in the given data.

   (e) Maps help us understand locations and help us see how big or small places are in comparison to other places. This can be done using scale.

   (f) A key tells us the meaning of different symbols used in a map.

   (g) Maps also show direction.

Multiple Choice Questions

A B C D

(1-2): The graph shows the number of students who attended a book fair.

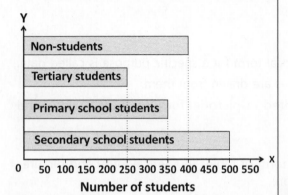

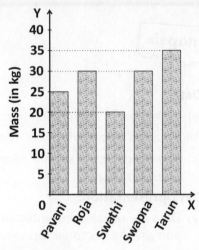

1 Twice the number of which students is the number of secondary school students?

(A) Tertiary students
(B) Non-students
(C) Primary school students
(D) Both (B) and (C)

2 If $\frac{1}{5}$ of the primary school students were below 10 years old, how many primary school students were 10 years old and above?

(A) 210   (B) 350
(C) 140   (D) 280

(3-5): The bar graph shows the mass of 5 children.

3 What is the difference in the mass of the heaviest child and the lightest child?

(A) 10 kg   (B) ·15 kg
(C) 0 kg   (D) 5 kg

4 Which of the two children have the same mass?

(A) Swapna and Swathi
(B) Roja and Swathi
(C) Roja and Swapna
(D) Pavani and Tarun

5 Who is 15 kg heavier than Swathi?

(A) Tarun   (B) Swapna
(C) Roja   (D) Pavani

(6-7): The graph shows the marks obtained by five students in a mathematics test.

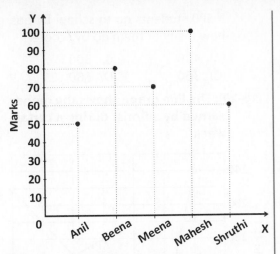

6 Who got $\frac{3}{4}$ of Beena's marks?

(A) Anil   (B) Mahesh
(C) Shruthi   (D) Meena

7 What is the average marks obtained by the five pupils?

(A) 70   (B) 75
(C) 72   (D) 62

8 The pie-chart shows the games played by a group of boys.

Games played by a group of boys

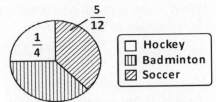

Based on the information given in the pie-chart, which of the following statements is true?

(A) $\frac{1}{3}$ of the number of boys play badminton.

(B) $\frac{1}{8}$ of the number of boys play hockey.

(C) 50% of the boys play hockey.

(D) 40% of the boys play hockey.

(9-10): The bar graph shows Vikram's savings in 6 months.

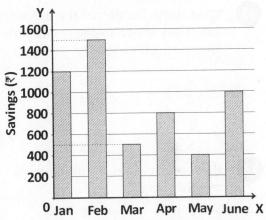

Vikram's monthly salary is ₹ 2500.

9 What percent of his salary did he spend in January?

(A) 52%   (B) 28%
(C) 48%   (D) 20.5%

10 In which month did he spend twice as much as in February?

(A) January   (B) March
(C) June   (D) April

(11-13): The graph shows how Jatin spends his pocket money each month.

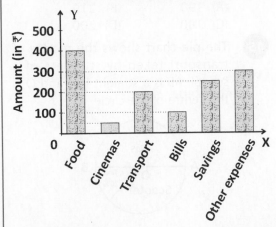

11 How many times the amount spent on cinemas is the amount spent on transport?

(A) 4   (B) 2
(C) 1   (D) 3

12 What is the fraction of the amount spent on other expenses to the amount spent on food?

(A) $\dfrac{2}{3}$ (B) $\dfrac{3}{4}$

(C) $\dfrac{3}{5}$ (D) $\dfrac{1}{3}$

13 How much does Jatin earn per month?

(A) ₹ 1050   (B) ₹ 1200
(C) ₹ 1250   (D) ₹ 1300

14 The pie-chart shows the number of fruits in a fruit stall.

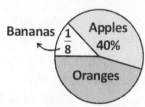

If there are 210 apples and bananas at the stall, how many oranges are there?

(A) 190   (B) 210
(C) 180   (D) 200

15 The pie-chart shows the modes of transport taken by students of a school. AB is a straight line and O is the centre of the circle.

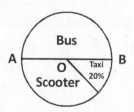

If 500 students go to school by bus, how many of them go by scooter?

(A) 400   (B) 300
(C) 360   (D) 180

(16-20): The line graph shows the money earned by a florist during a certain week.

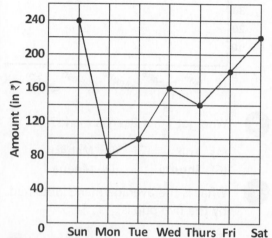

16 On which day did he earn ₹ 100 more than the amount earned on Monday?

(A) Tuesday   (B) Wednesday
(C) Thursday   (D) Friday

17 What is the average amount earned from Sunday to Wednesday?

(A) ₹ 120   (B) ₹ 142.50
(C) ₹ 145   (D) ₹ 157.50

18 On which day was his earnings $\dfrac{4}{5}$ of his earnings on Tuesday?

(A) Monday   (B) Wednesday
(C) Thursday   (D) Friday

19 On which two days did the florist earn a total amount equal to the amount earned on Friday?

(A) Sunday, Monday
(B) Monday, Tuesday
(C) Tuesday, Thursday
(D) Wednesday, Saturday

9. Data Handling

20 Find the ratio of the amount earned on weekdays to that on weekends.

(A) 23 : 33   (B) 3 : 2
(C) 33 : 23   (D) 2 : 3

(21-22): The line graph shows the time taken by 5 boys to run a race.

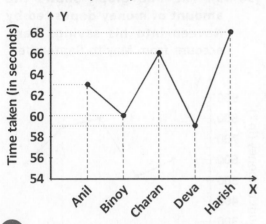

21 What is the average time taken by the boys to complete the race?

(A) 62.5 seconds (B) 63.2 seconds
(C) 64 seconds   (D) 63 seconds

22 What is the difference in time taken by Deva and Harish to complete the race?

(A) 8 seconds   (B) 2 seconds
(C) 9 seconds   (D) 5 seconds

(23-25): The pie-chart given shows the distribution of Maya's allowance for a certain month. AB is the diameter.

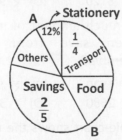

23 What fraction of her allowance was not spent on stationery?

(A) $\dfrac{3}{25}$ (B) $\dfrac{2}{5}$

(C) $\dfrac{4}{5}$ (D) $\dfrac{22}{25}$

24 Maya deposited 50% of her savings in the bank. If she deposited ₹ 120 in the bank, what was her monthly allowance?

(A) ₹ 240   (B) ₹ 600
(C) ₹ 480   (D) ₹ 300

25 The ratio of amount of money that Maya spent on food to the amount of money she spent on transport is 9 : 10. If she spent the same amount on transport each month, how much did she spend on transport in a year?

(A) ₹ 1440   (B) ₹ 108
(C) ₹ 1296   (D) ₹ 120

(26-28): Students of class 5 were asked to choose their favourite fruit. The given pie-chart shows their choices.

26 If 10 students chose apple as their favourite fruit, how many students chose chickoo?

(A) 9   (B) 15
(C) 6   (D) 8

27 What is the ratio of the number of students who chose the most popular fruit to the number of students who chose the least popular fruit?

(A) 5 : 2   (B) 2 : 5
(C) 1 : 3   (D) 3 : 1

9. Data Handling

28 How many students were there in class 5 if 10 of them liked apple?

(A) 20   (B) 30
(C) 40   (D) 50

(29-33): The bar graph given shows the mathematics marks obtained by 40 pupils.

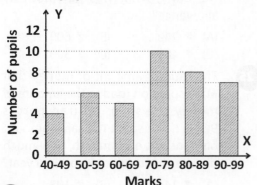

29 What fraction of pupils scored below 60 marks?

(A) $\dfrac{1}{5}$ (B) $\dfrac{1}{4}$

(C) $\dfrac{1}{3}$ (D) $\dfrac{2}{5}$

30 A pupil passed the exam if he scored 50 marks and above. Find the ratio of the number of pupils who passed to the number of pupils who failed.

(A) 9 : 1   (B) 2 : 9
(C) 1 : 9   (D) 9 : 2

31 A pupil who scored 80 marks and above is awarded Honors grade. What percentage of pupils secured the Honors grade?

(A) 43.5%   (B) 62.5%
(C) 57.5%   (D) 37.5%

32 How many pupils scored the least marks?

(A) 4   (B) 8
(C) 6   (D) 7

33 Identify the ratio of the number of pupils who scored 70-79 marks to those who scored 80-89.

(A) 4 : 5   (B) 5 : 2
(C) 2 : 5   (D) 5 : 4

(34-35): The line graph shows the amount of money deposited by Naveen into his savings bank account from May to September.

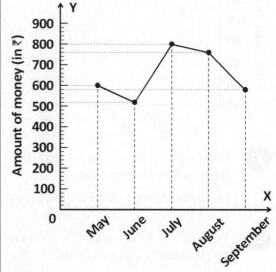

34 At the end of April, Naveen had ₹ 6200 in his savings account. How much money did he have at the end of July?

(A) ₹ 4270   (B) ₹ 7320
(C) ₹ 8120   (D) ₹ 9470

35 How much amount of money did Naveen save from May to September?

(A) ₹ 1120   (B) ₹ 1930
(C) ₹ 2680   (D) ₹ 3260

36 The pie-chart shows the number of different flowers sold by a florist.

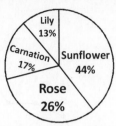

How much more percent of sun flowers than lilies did the florist sell?

(A) $238\dfrac{6}{13}$%   (B) 31%

(C) $236\dfrac{8}{13}$%   (D) 57%

37 The pie-chart shows the number of different colour T-shirts sold by Dinesh on a particular day.

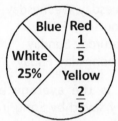

If he sold 1400 yellow T-shirts on that day, how many blue T-shirts did he sell?

(A) 1200   (B) 615
(C) 525   (D) 635

38 The pie-chart shows the various types of fruits used to make a bowl of salad.

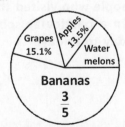

What percentage of fruits used are watermelons?

(A) 21.4%   (B) 60%
(C) 12%   (D) 11.4%

(39-42): The pie-chart shows the number of vehicles in a car park. The total number of vehicles in the car park is 7000. AB is the diameter.

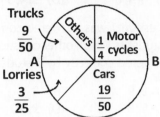

39 How many lorries are there in the car park?
(A) 840   (B) 860
(C) 480   (D) 820

40 If 30% of the 'Others' are cycles, how many cycles are there?
(A) 117   (B) 28
(C) 147   (D) 49

41 What is the ratio of the number of trucks to that of lorries?
(A) 1:4   (B) 3:2
(C) 3:1   (D) 2:3

42 How many more cars were parked than motor cycles?
(A) 910   (B) 810
(C) 900   (D) 1010

(43-48): The bar graph shows the results of some students who took a mathematics quiz.

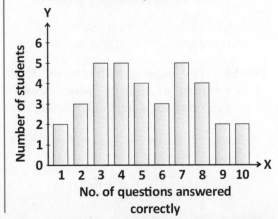

43 Which three questions were answered correctly by 5 students?

(A) 3, 4, 7   (B) 2, 3, 4
(C) 3, 4, 8   (D) 3, 4, 5

44 Question 1 was answered correctly by 2 students. Which other questions were answered correctly by 2 students?

(A) 8, 9   (B) 3, 4
(C) 5, 8   (D) 9, 10

45 How many fewer students answered question 1 correctly than question 4?

(A) 1   (B) 3
(C) 4   (D) 2

46 What is the ratio of the number of students who answered questions 2 and 6 correctly to that who answered questions 5 and 8 correctly?

(A) 2 : 3   (B) 5 : 3
(C) 3 : 4   (D) 4 : 3

47 Which of the following is the number of questions answered correctly by the same number of students?

(A) 2, 5   (B) 3, 7
(C) 5, 9   (D) 2, 10

48 What percent of questions were answered correctly by 5 students?

(A) 13%   (B) 30%
(C) 27%   (D) 33%

(49-50): The line graph shows the amount of money Sonu saved each day for a particular week.

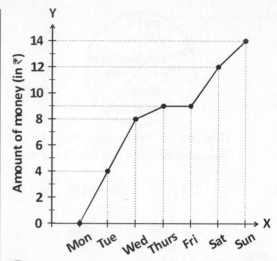

49 On which two days did Sonu save the same amount of money?

(A) Tuesday, Wednesday
(B) Thursday, Friday
(C) Saturday, Sunday
(D) Wednesday, Friday

50 What is the average amount of money saved by Sonu in the given week?

(A) ₹ 8   (B) ₹ 8.10
(C) ₹ 56   (D) ₹ 9

 Previous Contest Questions

(1-3): The bar graph shows the number of people who visited the science fair in a particular school from Monday to Friday.

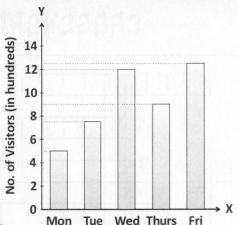

1 What is the percentage increase in the number of visitors on Tuesday than on Wednesday?

(A) 10%   (B) 37.5%
(C) 60%   (D) 67%

2 How many visitors visited the fair on the given 5 days?

(A) 4500   (B) 4600
(C) 4200   (D) 4100

3 What is the average number of visitors per day rounded to the nearest hundred?

(A) 950   (B) 920
(C) 1000   (D) 900

(4-10): The line graph given shows the amount of money collected from a charity drive over 5 weeks.

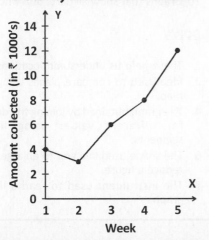

4 What is the amount of money collected in the 3rd week?

(A) ₹ 6000   (B) ₹ 4000
(C) ₹ 3000   (D) ₹ 8000

5 How much was collected over the period of 5 weeks?

(A) ₹ 33   (B) ₹ 33000
(C) ₹ 3300   (D) ₹ 30000

6 What is the ratio of increase in the amount of money collected in 2nd and 3rd weeks to that in 4th and 5th weeks?

(A) 3 : 4   (B) 3 : 2
(C) 4 : 3   (D) 1 : 3

7 What is the average weekly amount of money collected?

(A) ₹ 5000   (B) ₹ 5600
(C) ₹ 6600   (D) ₹ 6000

8 In which week was the least amount of money collected?

(A) 1st week   (B) 2nd week
(C) 5th week   (D) 3rd week

9 What percentage of the amount of money collected in the 5th week is the amount of money collected in the 1st week?

(A) $33\frac{1}{3}$%   (B) 33%

(C) 34%   (D) 30%

10 Between which two consecutive weeks is the increase in amount of money collected the maximum?

(A) 2 and 3   (B) 1 and 2
(C) 4 and 5   (D) 3 and 4

9. Data Handling

CROSSWORD

8. Measurement

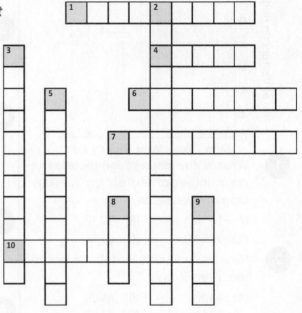

ACROSS

1 1 lakh centimtres.
4 The basic unit of capacity.
6 The operation used to change a smaller unit to a bigger unit.
7 100 decalitres.
10 The process that helps in comparison.

DOWN

2 The operation used to change a bigger unit to a smaller unit.
3 Measure of a dose of medicinal syrup.
5 A tenth of a centimetre.
8 10 decigrams.
9 1000 kilograms.

9. Data Handling

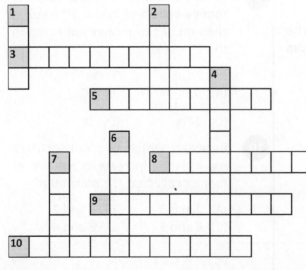

ACROSS

3 The pictorial representation of data, using symbols.
5 This can be found using maps.
8 The graph drawn using rectangles.
9 The lines used to count the number.
10 Graphs that show all parts of a whole.

DOWN

1 These help us understand locations.
2 Idea used to compare places using a map.
4 The graph obtained by joining the dots for different values using line segments.
6 The shape used in a grid to enlarge or reduce a figure.
7 The instrument used to read a line graph.

Questions@stimulating-minds

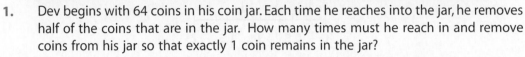

1. Dev begins with 64 coins in his coin jar. Each time he reaches into the jar, he removes half of the coins that are in the jar. How many times must he reach in and remove coins from his jar so that exactly 1 coin remains in the jar?

   (A) 5   (B) 32   (C) 6   (D) 7

2. For every 3 chocolates that Simran buys at the regular price, she buys a fourth chocolate for ₹ 5. Simran buys 12 chocolates in total for ₹ 105. What is the regular price of one chocolate, in rupees?

   (A) 100   (B) 45   (C) 10   (D) 90

3. The rectangle shown has side lengths of 8 and 4. What is the area of the shaded region?

   (A) 32   (B) 16   (C) 64   (D) 12

4. The sum of four numbers is T. Suppose that each of the four numbers is now increased by 1. These four new numbers are added together and then the sum is tripled. What is the value of this final result?

   (A) 3T + 3   (B) 3T + 4   (C) 3T + 12   (D) T + 12

5. Recycling 1 tonne of paper will save 24 trees. If 4 schools each recycle $\frac{3}{4}$ of a tonne of paper, how many total number of trees this will save?

   (A) 24   (B) 72   (C) 18   (D) 126

6. In the given figure, the square has a perimeter of 48 and the triangle has a height of 48. If the square and the triangle have the same area, what is the value of x?

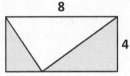

   (A) 1.5   (B) 12   (C) 6   (D) 3

7. In the multiplication shown, P, Q and R are all different digits so that

$$\begin{array}{r} P\ P\ Q \\ \times\qquad Q \\ \hline R\ Q\ 5\ Q \end{array}$$

   What is the value of P + Q + R?

   (A) 20   (B) 13   (C) 15   (D) 17

8. In the given figure, w, x, y and z represent numbers in the intervals indicated. Which fraction represents the largest value?

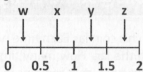

(A) $\dfrac{x}{w}$　　　　(B) $\dfrac{y}{x}$　　　　(C) $\dfrac{y}{w}$　　　　(D) $\dfrac{z}{w}$

9. Last year, Kriti's age was a multiple of 7. This year, Kritis age is a multiple of 5. In how many years will Kriti be 26 years old?

(A) 11　　　　(B) 21　　　　(C) 4　　　　(D) 18

10. A square has perimeter 24. A rectangle has the same area as the square. If the width of the rectangle is 4, What is the perimeter of the rectangle?

(A) 26　　　　(B) 36　　　　(C) 16　　　　(D) 32

11. The points A, B, C, D and E represent values along the given number line. A, B, C and D are between 0 and 1, and E is between 1 and 2. Which point best represents the value of B × C?

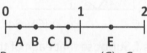

(A) A　　　　(B) B　　　　(C) C　　　　(D) D

12. Goutham has a collection of 50 songs that are each 3 minutes in length and 50 songs that are each 5 minutes in length. What is the maximum number of songs from his collection that he can play in 3 hours?

(A) 100　　　　(B) 36　　　　(C) 56　　　　(D) 60

13. There are a certain number of red balls, green balls and blue balls in a bag. Of the balls in the bag, $\dfrac{1}{3}$ are red and $\dfrac{2}{7}$ are blue. The number of green balls in the bag is 8 less than twice the number of blue balls. Find the number of green balls in the bag.

(A) 12　　　　(B) 16　　　　(C) 20　　　　(D) 24

14. A class of 30 students recently wrote a test. If 20 students scored 80, 8 students scored 90, and 2 students scored 100, find the class average on this test.

(A) 90　　　　(B) 84　　　　(C) 82　　　　(D) 86

15. In the multiplication shown, P and Q each represent a single digit, and the product is 32 951. What is the value of P + Q?

$$\begin{array}{r} 3\;9\;P \\ \times\;Q\;3 \\ \hline 3\;2\;9\;5\;1 \end{array}$$

(A) 14　　　　(B) 12　　　　(C) 15　　　　(D) 13

16. The 6 members of an executive committee want to call a meeting. Each of them phones 6 different people, who in turn each calls 6 other people. If no one is called more than once, how many people will know about the meeting?

    (A) 18   (B) 36   (C) 216   (D) 258

17. If the area of the shaded part of the square is 16, then the perimeter of the square is

    (A) 8   (B) 16   (C) 32   (D) 64

18. Six friends ate at a restaurant and agreed tos hare the bill equally. Because Lakshmi forgot her money, each of her five friends paid an extra ₹ 3 to cover her portion of the total bill. What was the total bill?

    (A) ₹ 90   (B) ₹ 84   (C) ₹ 75   (D) ₹ 108

19. The different between 19 992 000 and some smaller whole number equals the difference between some larger whole number and 19 992 000. The average of the smaller and larger whole numbers is

    (A) 6 664 000   (B) 9 996 000   (C) 19 992 000   (D) 39 984 000

20. My clock set correctly at 6 p.m., gained 5 minutes each true hour. When my clock next read 7 a.m., I gave my friend a wake-up call and discovered that the correct time was ____ a.m.

    (A) 5: 55   (B) 6   (C) 6: 55   (D) 8: 05

Model Test Paper

1 The solid given is made up of 1 m cubes.

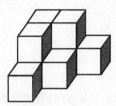

What is its volume?

(A) 9 m³   (B) 9 cm³
(C) 90 cm³   (D) 90 m³

2 Study the prime factorisation of X and Y given.

$$X = 2 \times 3 \times 3 \times 3 \times 3 \times 3 \times 5$$

$$Y = 2 \times 2 \times 3 \times 3 \times 5 \times 19$$

What is the place value of 8 in the sum of the numbers X and Y?

(A) 8 × 1000   (B) 8 × 100
(C) 8 × 10   (D) 8 × 1

3 How many right angles are there in the figure given?

(A) 2   (B) 3
(C) 0   (D) 4

4 If 30% of ₹ 60 is spent, find the remaining amount.

(A) ₹ 18   (B) ₹ 36
(C) ₹ 42   (D) ₹ 30

5 What is the place value of 3 in 712,364,962?

(A) Hundred thousand
(B) 300 thousands
(C) 3 millions
(D) 3

6 Hema is 3 kg heavier than Kamala, who is 2 kg lighter than Monica. How much heavier is Hema than Monica?

(A) 3 kg   (B) 1.5 kg
(C) 1 kg   (D) 2 kg

7 What is the product obtained when $\frac{11}{12}, \frac{16}{4}$ and $\frac{9}{16}$ are multiplied?

(A) $1\frac{2}{15}$ (B) $2\frac{1}{4}$

(C) $2\frac{1}{16}$ (D) $\frac{33}{48}$

8 The pie-chart shows the number of fruits in a fruit stall.

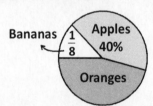

If there are 210 apples and bananas at the stall, how many oranges are there?

(A) 190   (B) 210
(C) 180   (D) 200

9 Which type of numbers have only 1 and itself as factors?

(A) Composite numbers
(B) Even numbers
(C) Prime numbers
(D) Odd numbers

10 Which of the following is the least length?

(A) 130 cm   (B) 0.72 m
(C) 0.12 m   (D) 84 cm

11 Identify the product when 7.854 is multiplied by 10.

(A) 785.4   (B) 78.54
(C) 7854   (D) 78540

12 Which of the following shapes cannot be tessellated?

(A)   (B)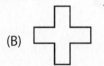

(C)   (D)

13 The perimeter of a square desk is 2 m. What is its area?

(A) 25 m²   (B) 2500 cm²
(C) 2500 cm   (D) 25 cm²

14 340264 is the same as 300000 + ☐ + 200 + 60 + 4. What is the missing number in the box?

(A) 400   (B) 40000
(C) 4000   (D) 400000

15 What is the length of a ribbon which is 90% of 300 m?

(A) 27 m   (B) 207 m
(C) 270 m   (D) 272 m

16 The L.C.M. of two numbers is 10 times their H.C.F. Find the numbers.

(A) 24, 96   (B) 16, 15
(C) 24, 480   (D) 24, 240

17 Observe the given number line.

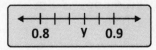

Which decimal number does 'y' represent?

(A) 0.83   (B) 0.85
(C) 0.86   (D) 0.88

18 How does the measure of an angle change when one of its arms is extended?

(A) Doubles
(B) Increases proportionately
(C) Decreases proportionately
(D) Remains the same

19 Observe the following.

$$\frac{5}{20} = \frac{9}{?}$$

What is the missing number in the box?

(A) 24   (B) 36
(C) 33   (D) 20

20 The figure given shows 5 numbers.

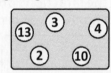

Which of the 5 numbers are the prime factors of 130?

(A) 2 and 3   (B) 10 and 13
(C) 2 and 13   (D) 3 and 10

21 A tree is 15 m tall. A flag pole is $\frac{3}{5}$ as tall as the tree. What is their total height?

(A) 9 m   (B) 15 m
(C) 48 m   (D) 24 m

22 Find the edge of a cube whose volume is 27 cu cm.

(A) $\frac{1}{9}$ cm   (B) $\frac{1}{3}$ cm

(C) 3 cm   (D) 9 cm

23 Under which period in the place value chart is ten millions?

(A) Crores   (B) Lakhs
(C) Thousands   (D) Millions

24 There are 100 questions on Manu's test. She has completed 40 of the questions. What percent of the questions has Manu completed ?

(A) 0.4%   (B) 4%
(C) 40%   (D) 400%

25 Rajesh's pocket money is ₹ 7.50 per day. He spends ₹ 1.30 per day and saves the rest. How much does he save in the month of April 2013?

(A) ₹ 176   (B) ₹ 186
(C) ₹ 196   (D) ₹ 206

26 Estimate the temperature on a cool winter day.

(A) 35 °C   (B) 40 °C
(C) 27 °C   (D) 20 °C

27 Find the fraction obtained on evaluating the given expression.

$$1\frac{1}{2} + \frac{3}{4} \times \frac{6}{3} \div \frac{1}{4}$$

(A) $2\frac{1}{2}$ (B) $3\frac{1}{2}$

(C) $7\frac{1}{2}$ (D) $8\frac{1}{2}$

28 The figure given is made up of 2 similar squares X and Y.

X	Y

Find the perimeter of the figure, if the area of square X is 49 cm².

(A) 14 cm   (B) 42 cm
(C) 7 cm   (D) 21 cm

29 Which of the following is the resultant of 76823 rounded to the nearest thousands?

(A) 76000   (B) 75000
(C) 77000   (D) 78000

30 Observe the following.

$$4 \div 1000 = 0.4 \div \boxed{?}$$

What is the missing number in the box?

(A) 10   (B) 100
(C) 1000   (D) 10000

31 What is 0.1% equal to?

(A) $\frac{1}{10}$ (B) $\frac{1}{100}$

(C) $\frac{1}{1000}$ (D) $\frac{1}{10000}$

32 Which of the following cannot be prime factorised?

(A) Even numbers
(B) Odd numbers
(C) Prime numbers
(D) Composite numbers

33 The radius of a circle is 7 cm. What is its diameter?

(A) 14 cm   (B) 3.5 cm
(C) 10 cm   (D) 7 cm

34 There were 15 l of oil in a can. A certain amount of oil is used to fill up 4 bottles each of capacity 0.5 l. How many similar bottles are needed to fill up the remaining oil?

(A) 13   (B) 26
(C) 39   (D) 42

35 How is the expression 100 – 7 × 1 + 5 written using brackets?

(A) (100 – 7) × (1 + 5)
(B) (100 – 7) × 1 + 5
(C) 100 – 7 × (1 + 5)
(D) 100 – (7 × 1) + 5

36 Find the missing number.

$$5 : 9 = 45 : \boxed{?}$$

(A) 81   (B) 40
(C) 5   (D) 14

37 A rectangular field has a perimeter of 64 m. The ratio of its length to its breadth is 5 : 3. Find the area of the field.

(A) 120 m²   (B) 360 m²
(C) 240 m²   (D) 480 m²

38 Water in a vessel is at a temperature of 38.5 °C. By how much its temperature must be increased so as to boil it?

(A) 38.5 °C   (B) 100 °C
(C) 61.5 °C   (D) 82.5 °C

39 What is the H.C.F. of 120, 144 and 216?

(A) 38   (B) 24
(C) 120   (D) 144

40 How many thousandths more than 7.04 is 7.54?

(A) 5   (B) 50
(C) 500   (D) 5000

41 Observe the given decimal numbers.

0.87	0.453	0.72
	0.207	

Which is the correct ascending order of the given decimals?

(A) 0.87, 0.72, 0.453, 0.207
(B) 0.72, 0.453, 0.87, 0.207
(C) 0.453, 0.72, 0.87, 0.207
(D) 0.207, 0.453, 0.72, 0.87

42 Find the sum of $2\frac{1}{2}$ and $\frac{1}{3}$.

(A) $2\frac{1}{5}$ (B) $2\frac{5}{6}$

(C) $2\frac{1}{6}$ (D) $2\frac{3}{5}$

43 27th February 2014 was a Wednesday. What day was 27th March, the same year?

(A) Sunday   (B) Wednesday
(C) Monday   (D) Friday

44 Which of the following is the set of Roman numerals used to write the equivalent of 2014?

(A) M, X, V, I   (B) D, X, L, I
(C) M, D, L, V   (D) M, L, X

45 In the given figure, what is the value of $\angle y$?

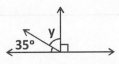

(A) 45°   (B) 55°
(C) 90°   (D) 65°

(46-47): The line graph shows the time taken by 5 boys to run a race.

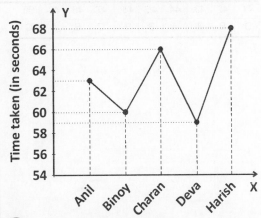

46 What is the average time taken by the boys to complete the race?

(A) 62.5 seconds (B) 63.2 seconds
(C) 64 seconds   (D) 63 seconds

47 What is the difference in time taken by Deva and Harish to complete the race?

(A) 8 seconds   (B) 2 seconds
(C) 9 seconds   (D) 5 seconds

48 Observe the following.

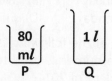

What is the ratio of the capacities of containers P and Q?

(A) 25 : 2   (B) 2 : 25
(C) 4 : 25   (D) 1 : 25

49 Which of the following is NOT a pair of twin primes?

(A) (23, 29)   (B) (11, 13)
(C) (59, 61)   (D) (71, 73)

50 Identify the correct equation.

(A) $6 + \dfrac{3}{1000} + \dfrac{6}{100} = 6.36$

(B) $0.6 = \dfrac{5}{8}$

(C) $\dfrac{6}{10} = 0.6$

(D) $0.003 = \dfrac{3}{100}$

Key

1	2	3	4	5	6	7	8	9	10	11	12	13	14	15	16	17	18	19	20
A	B	D	C	B	C	C	A	C	C	B	C	B	B	C	D	C	D	B	C

21	22	23	24	25	26	27	28	29	30	31	32	33	34	35	36	37	38	39	40
D	C	A	C	B	D	C	B	C	B	C	C	A	B	D	A	C	C	B	C

41	42	43	44	45	46	47	48	49	50
D	B	B	A	B	B	C	B	A	C

Explanatory Answers

1. Large Numbers

👉 **Multiple Choice Questions**

1. (C)

7	6	5	4	3	2	1
T.L	L	T.Th	Th	H	T	O

2. (B)

8	7	6	5	4	3	2	1
TM	M	H.Th	T.Th	Th	H	T	O

3. (C) The place value of 0 in any place in a number is zero.

4. (B) Their sum = 100000000 + 99999999 = 199999999

5. (B) The required difference =

$$\begin{array}{r} 9999999 \\ -\ \ \ 10000 \\ \hline 9989999 \end{array}$$

6. (C) The place values of the digits increase by 10 times from right to left in a number.

7. (B)

Indian system		C	TL	L	T.Th	Th	H	T	O
International system	TM	M	H.Th	T.Th	Th	H	T	O

Hence, 10 million = 1 crore.

8. (B) 9. (C) 10. (B) 11. (A)

12. (D) The missing digit according to the given expansion is 7.

13. (B) The value of 8 in the ten thousands place is 80000 = 80 × 1000
= 1000 times the value of 8 in the tens place

14. (C) 5842 × 49 ≈ 5800 × 50 = 290000

15. (C) The smallest 7-digit number is 10,00,000
= The successor of the greatest 6-digit number
= The greatest 6-digit number + 1

16. (A) The place value of 5 in 9125678 is 5000. Its face value is 5. Thus, the required difference = 5000 – 5 = 4995.

17. (C) 792 × 650 = (800 – 8) × 650
= 800 × 650 – $\boxed{8}$ × $\boxed{650}$

∴ The value of the product of the missing numbers is 8 × 650 = 5200.

18. (B) The smallest 6-digit odd number = 100001
The largest 4-digit even number = 9998
Their difference = 100001 – 9998 = 90003

19. (A) 20. (B) 21. (D)

22. (A) The greatest 6-digit odd number that can be formed using 6,0,3,7,6 and 9 is 976603.
The difference in place values of the two 6's in 976603 is 6000 – 600 = 5400.

23. (A) 75 × 100 = 75 × 20 × 5

24. (D) 9232 km rounded to the nearest 1000 is 9000 km. Thus the reading of the odometer is 9 thousand kilometres.

25. (B) 100 ten thousands = 100 × 10000
= 1000000
65 thousands = 65000
50 hundreds = 5000
2 ones = 2
∴ The required value is 1000000 + 65000 + 5000 + 2 = 1070002.

26. (B) The product of 255 and 37 is
255 × 37 = 9435
The place value of 9 in 9435 is 9000
= 90 × 100
Thus, 9 stands for 90 hundreds.

27. (A) The numbers that result in 223000 when a rounded off to the nearest thousand are 222500 to 223499. The largest among them is 223499.

28. (D) From the given number line, the difference between every two consecutive markings is 20.
So, X = 3006960 and Y = 3007000.
Therefore, the required difference is Y – X = 3007000 – 3006960 = 40.

29. (B) 1 million = 1,000,000
30 thousands = 30,000
The required number
= 1,000,000 – 30,000
= 970,000
= 9700 × 100
9700 hundreds must be added to 30 thousands to get 1 million.

30. (D)

L	T.Th	Th	H	T	O
4	3	8	4	9	8

The sum of the values of 8 in 438498 is
8000 + 8 = 8008.

31. (C) According to the problem,
M = 63549 and N = 149500.
Their sum = 63549 + 149500 = 213049

32. (C)   **33.** (C)   **34.** (C)

35. (B) In 178762, the digit in tens place is
6 > 5. So, 178762 rounded to the nearest
hundreds is 178800.

36. (D) 38,65,62,048

The digit in ten thousands place is
6 > 5.

So, 38,65,62,048 rounded to the nearest
lakhs is 38,66,00,000.

37. (B) The required smaller number
= 8765432 − 174325 = 8591107

38. (D) Total number of students and teachers
= 2476

No. of teachers and boys = 1289

∴ No. of girls = 2476 − 1289 = 1187

No. of girls and teachers = 1246

∴ No. of boys = 2476 − 1246 = 1230

Total no. of boys and girls
= 1187 + 1230 = 2417

Hence, the number of teachers
= 2476 − 2417 = 59

☞ **Previous Contest Questions**

1. (D) 1753 = 1000 + 500 + 100 + 100 + 50 + 1
+ 1 + 1 = MDCCLIII

2. (A) DCLV = 500 + 100 + 50 + 5 = 655
XLVI = (50 − 10) + 5 + 1 = 46
MDCL = 1000 + 500 + 100 + 50
       = 1650 ≠ 1560
So, only (i) and (ii) are correct.

3. (C) ML = 1000 + 50 = 1050
LX = 50 + 10 = 60
CLV = 100 + 50 + 5 = 155
XL = 50 − 10 = 40
∴ P has the largest number.

4. (B) 29 = 30 − 1 = 10 + 10 + (10 − 1) = XXIX
∴ No. of match sticks needed = 7

5. (A) 1618 = 1000 + 500 + 100 + 10 + 5 + 1 +
1 + 1 = MDCXVIII

6. (B) CDCX = (500 − 100) + 100 + 10
      = 400 + 110 = 510
CDXL = (500 − 100) + (50 − 10) = 440
DCLX = 500 + 100 + 50 + 10 = 660
DCXL = 500 + 100 + (50 − 10) = 640
∴ CDXL has the least value.

7. (D) In evaluation of a numerical
expression, division (D), multiplication
(M), addition (A) and subtraction (S)
have to be performed in order.

8. (B) 30 × 8 ÷ 2 + 62 − 24
= 30 × 4 + 62 − 24
= 120 + 62 − 24
= 182 − 24 = 158

9. (C) 909000 ÷ 9090 = 159 − $\boxed{?}$

100 = 159 − $\boxed{?}$

∴ The missing number is 159 − 100 = 59

10. (D) 100 − 7 × 1 + 5

According to DMAS, as multiplication
has to be carried out before addition
and subtraction, the given expression
can be written as 100 − (7 × 1) + 5.

2. Factors and Multiples

☞ **Multiple Choice Questions**

1. (B)   **2.** (A)

3. (D) Multiples of 10: 10, 20, 30, 40, 50, ⓺⓪, 70, ...

Multiples of 12: 12, 24, 36, 48, ⓺⓪, 72, ...

∴ The smallest whole number divisible
by both 10 and 12 is 60.

4. (B)   **5.** (C)

6. (A) L.C.M. of 12 and 18 is 36.

∴ The required number of stamps is
the largest multiple of 36, less than 500.

500 ÷ 36 = 13 R 32 as

36 × 13 = 468 and 36 × 14 = 504.

Thus, the required number of stamps
= 468

7. (C) Co-prime numbers have no common
factor other than 1. So, their L.C.M. is
their product.

8. (A)

Divisors	12	24	36
720	60	30	20
1080	90	45	30
1440	120	60	40
2160	180	90	60
5760	480	240	160

Hence, 23 is not the divisor of the given number as it does not divide any of them exactly.

9. (C) $12 = ② \times ② \times ③$

$24 = ② \times ② \times 2 \times ③$

$36 = ② \times ② \times ③ \times 3$

L. C. M. of 12, 24 and 36

$= 2 \times 2 \times 3 \times 2 \times 3 = 72$

10. (B) The prime numbers that differ by 2 are called twin primes.

e.g., 3, 5 as both 3 and 5 are prime numbers and their difference is 2.

11. (A) Factors of 36 are ①, ②, ③, ④, ⑥, ⑨, ⑫, ⑱ and ㊱.

Factors of 144 are ①, ②, ③, ④, ⑥, 8, ⑨, ⑫, 16, ⑱, 24, ㊱, 48, 72 and 144.

The common factors of 36 and 144 are 1, 2, 3, 4, 6, 9, 12, 18 and 36 of which 36 is the highest.

∴ H. C. F of 36 and 144 is 36.

12. (A) Co-prime numbers have no common factor other than 1. So, their H.C.F is 1.

13. (B) L. C. M. of 45 and 50 is

$5 \times 9 \times 10 = 450 = P$.

∴ $10P + 100 = 450 \times 10 + 100$

$= 4500 + 100 = 4600$

14. (A)   15. (C)   16. (A)   17. (B)

18. (C) The prime numbers between 50 and 100 are 53, 59, 61, 67, 71, 73, 79, 83, 89 and 97, which are 10 in number.

19. (C) 20 expressed as a product of primes is $2 \times 2 \times 5$.

20. (A) The L.C.M. of co-primes is their product.

21. (D) H.C.F. of 60, 650, 250 is 10.

H.C.F. of 230, 450 is 10.

H.C.F. of 120, 180, 240 is 60.

H.C.F. of 135, 315, 495 is 45.

Hence, P and Q have numbers with the same H.C.F.

22. (B) H.C.F. of 11, 33 and 88 is 11.

L.C.M. of 11, 33 and 88 is $11 \times 3 \times 8$

$= 11 \times 24 = $ H.C.F. $\times 24$

23. (A) Co-prime numbers are numbers that have no common factor other than 1.

24. (D) Let the numbers be 24 and 240.

Then their H.C.F. = 24

and L. C. M. = 240

Hence the required numbers are 24 and 240.

25. (D) The sum of the first five multiples of 8 is $8 + 16 + 24 + 32 + 40 = 120$.

26. (A) The least 4 – digit number is 1000, which is exactly divisible by 8 as $8 \times 125 = 1000$.

27. (B) Factors of 40 are 1, 2, 4, 5, 8, 10, 20, 40.

Their product is $1 \times 2 \times 4 \times 5 \times 8 \times 10 \times 20 \times 40 = 256 \times 10000 = 2560000$.

28. (A) The factors of 256 are 1, 2, 4, 8, 16, 32, 64, 128 and 256, which are 9 in number.

29. (D) Factors of 140 are 1, 2, 4, 5, 7, 10, 14, 20, 28, 35, 70 and 140.

Their sum $= 336 = 3 \times 100 + 36$

∴ The sum of the factors of 140 has 3 hundreds.

30. (A) Factors of 84 are 1, 2, 3, 4, 6, 7, 12, 14, 21, 28, 42 and 84.

Their sum $= 224$

So, the digits in hundreds and tens place are the same; i.e., 2.

31. (A)

```
5 | 2025
5 | 405
9 | 81
    9
```

$2025 = 5 \times 5 \times 9 \times 9$

$= A \times A \times B \times B$

Therefore, A = 5 and B = 9.

32. (D)

```
3 | 2145
5 | 715
11 | 143
     13
```

∴ $2145 = 3 \times 5 \times 11 \times 13$

(3, 5); (11, 13) are the twin primes, i.e., P and R are the required twin primes.

33. (A) The product of factors in the prime factorisation of a number $= (2 \times 2 \times 2) \times (3 \times 3 \times 3 \times 3) \times 5$

∴ The number = The product of the given prime factors = 3240

34. (C) According to the problem, the number of pens is exactly divisible by 18.

Also, the number is 5 less to be divisible by 19.

∴ The required number is $19 \times 5 - 5$

$= 95 - 5 = 90$, which is exactly divisible by 18

35. (D) Factors of 14 are 1, 2, 7 and 14.

Aakash's present age is a factor of 14 and his age the next year is a multiple of 5.

These conditions are satisfied for 14 as 14 is a factor of 14 and 1 more than 14 = 15 = multiple of 5.

Hence, in 6 years' time, the age of Aakash will be $14 + 6 = 20$ years.

36. (A) Factors of 42 : 1×42

2×21

3×14

6×7

The factors of 42, that are multiples of 7 are 7, 14, 21 and 42.

Their sum $= 7 + 14 + 21 + 42 = 84$

37. (A) Factors of 84 are 1, 2, 3, 4, 6, 7, 12, 14, 21, 26, 42 and 84.

Of these factors, multiples of 6 are 6, 12, 42 and 84.

∴ The required number is 42.

38. (D) Common factors of 36 and 24 are 1, 2, 3, 4, 6, 12.

P is the 2-digit common factor of 36 and 24.

∴ P = 12

Q is a factor and multiple of 28, which is 28.

∴ P + Q = 12 + 28 = 40

39. (A) $48 + 8 = 56 \div 14 = 4$.

∴ The required number is 48.

40. (A) The number is $5 \times 6 = 30$.

$30 \div 30 = 1$ is the required quotient.

41. (D) Twin primes between 1 and 100 are (3, 5), (5, 7), (11, 13), (17, 19), (29, 31), (41, 43), (59, 61) and (71, 73) which are 8 in number.

42. (B) 108240 has 2, 3, 4 and 10 as its factors as it is divisible by all of them.

43. (B) M = L. C. M. of 18, 24, 40 = 360

N = H. C. F of 60, 180, 360 = 60

∴ 2M + 15N = 1620

∴ The digit in thousands place is 1.

☞ **Previous Contest Questions**

1. (C) Common multiples of 4 and 5 are 20, 40 and 60, which are 3 in number within a minute.

2. (D) List all the prime numbers between 17 and 41. Then, find the value of p and q.

17, 19, 23, 28, 31, 37, 41.

∴ p = 23, q = 37

q − p = 37 − 23 = 14

3. (A) $136 \div 8 = 17$

$228 \div 8 = 28.5$

$842 \div 8 = 105.25$

$748 \div 2 = 93.5$

136 is exactly divisible by 8

Hence, 8 is a factor of 136.

4. (B)

3	3, 6,	x
2	1, 2,	$\frac{x}{3}$
$\frac{x}{6}$	1, 1,	$\frac{x}{6}$
	1, 1, 1	

Given that L.C.M. of 3, 6, × is 18,

∴ L.C.M. $= 3 \times 2 \times \dfrac{x}{6} = 18$, $\times = 18$.

5. (D) The factors of 81: ①, ③, ⑨, ㉗, 81

The factors of 108: ①, 2, ③, 4, 6, ⑨

12, 18, ㉗, 36, 54, 108

The highest common factor of 81 and 108 is 27.

∴ p + 3 = 27

p = 24.

6. (C) Multiples of 8 : 8, ⑯, 24, ..

Factors of 48: 1, 2, 3, 4, 6, 8, 12, ⑯, 24, 48

16 is both a multiple of 8 and a factor of 48.

7. (B)   8. (D)   9. (D)   10. (C)

3. Fractions

☞ **Multiple Choice Questions**

1. (C) Equivalent fraction of a given fraction is obtained by multiplying its numerator and denominator by the same number.

2. (A) On cross multiplication,

we get $9 \times 8 \boxed{\phantom{<}} 15 \times 16$

$$72 \boxed{<} 240$$

$$\therefore \frac{9}{16} < \frac{15}{8}$$

3. (B) $15\frac{2}{7} = \frac{15 \times 7 + 2}{7} = \frac{105 + 2}{7} = \frac{107}{7}$

4. (C) $\frac{45}{14} = 3\frac{3}{14}$

5. (D) $\frac{5}{13} + \frac{11}{13} + \frac{13}{13} = \frac{5 + 11 + 13}{13}$

$$= \frac{29}{13} = 2\frac{3}{13}$$

6. (A) The required number

$$= \frac{27}{25} - \frac{19}{25} = \frac{27 - 19}{25} = \frac{8}{25}$$

7. (A) $\frac{8}{4} + \frac{9}{6} + 1\frac{3}{5} = \frac{20 + 15 + 16}{10}$

$$= \frac{51}{10} = 5\frac{1}{10}$$

8. (B) The required difference

$$= \frac{23}{40} - \frac{9}{40} = \frac{14}{40}$$

9. (D) The numerator of a proper fraction is less than its denominator.

10. (C) Five - eighteenth $= \frac{5}{18}$

11. (A) Two complete rectangles and a half rectangle are shaded. So, the required fraction is $2\frac{1}{2}$.

12. (C) $4\frac{2}{3} = \frac{4 \times 3 + 2}{3} = \frac{14}{3}$

$\therefore$ Its reciprocal is $\frac{3}{14}$.

13. (B) The required product

$$= 1\frac{1}{3} \times 3\frac{1}{4} \times \frac{7}{8}$$

$$= \frac{4}{3} \times \frac{13}{4} \times \frac{7}{8}$$

$$= \frac{13 \times 7}{3 \times 8} = \frac{91}{24} = 3\frac{19}{24}$$

14. (D)   15. (B)

16. (A) Part of the book read $= \frac{3}{5}$

$\therefore$ Part of the book left to be read

$$= 1 - \frac{3}{5} = \frac{2}{5}$$

No. of pages left to be read $= 80$

$\therefore \frac{2}{5}$ part $= 80$

$\therefore$ No. of pages in the book

$$= 80 \times \frac{5}{2} = 40 \times 5 = 200$$

17. (A) Part of the cake Ravi had $= \frac{5}{6}$

Part of the Ravi's cake eaten $= \frac{2}{3}$

$\therefore$ Part of the cake eaten $= \frac{2}{3} \times \frac{5}{6} = \frac{5}{9}$

$\therefore$ Remaining part of the cake

$$= 1 - \frac{5}{9} = \frac{4}{9}$$

18. (D) Quantity of milk consumed in a day

$$= 3\frac{1}{2} \text{ litres}$$

No. of days in February 2013 $= 28$

$\therefore$ Quantity of milk consumed in February 2013 $= 3\frac{1}{2} \times 28 = 98$

19. (B) The product of a fraction and its reciprocal is 1.

20. (C) Reciprocals of 9 and $\frac{2}{9}$ are $\frac{1}{9}$ and $\frac{9}{2}$ respectively.

Their sum $= \frac{1}{9} + \frac{9}{2} = 4\frac{11}{18}$

21. (B) $\frac{1}{8} < \frac{1}{4}$. So, it should lie between 0 and $\frac{1}{4}$.

22. (B) Two out of 8 parts are shaded. So, the fraction is $\frac{2}{8} = \frac{1}{4}$.

23. (D) $11\frac{3}{5} \times 15 = \frac{58}{5} \times 15 = 58 \times 3$

24. (D) $2\dfrac{4}{5} = \dfrac{14}{5} = \dfrac{28}{10} = 28 \times \dfrac{1}{10}$

Hence, there are 28 tenths in $2\dfrac{4}{5}$.

25. (B) $\dfrac{2}{5} \rightarrow 48$

$\dfrac{1}{5} \rightarrow 48 \div 2 = 24$

$\dfrac{5}{5} = 24 \times 5 = 120$

$\therefore \dfrac{3}{5}$ of $120 = \dfrac{3}{5} \times 120 = 3 \times 24 = 72$

26. (C) No. of insects in the garden = 60

No. of ladybirds = 12

No. of butterflies $= \dfrac{1}{4} \times 60 = 15$

No. of ants = [60 – (12 + 15)] = 33

$\therefore$ The required fraction

$= \dfrac{\text{No. of ants}}{\text{Total no. of insects}} = \dfrac{33}{60} = \dfrac{11}{20}$

27. (D) Convert all fractions to those with the same denominators and compare their numerators.

$\therefore$ The fraction greater than $\dfrac{7}{8}$ is $\dfrac{11}{12}$.

28. (D) Mass of a packet of soil = Mass of a flower pot $+ 4\dfrac{1}{5}$ kg

$= 13\dfrac{1}{3}$ kg $+ 4\dfrac{1}{5}$ kg $= 17\dfrac{8}{15}$ kg

Total mass $= 13\dfrac{1}{3}$ kg $+ 17\dfrac{8}{15}$ kg

$= 30\dfrac{13}{15}$ kg

29. (C) Observing the given pattern, we find that the two fractions in a row add up to the one on its top row

i.e., $\dfrac{1}{2} + \dfrac{1}{4} = \dfrac{3}{4}$ and $\dfrac{1}{4} + \dfrac{1}{5} = \dfrac{9}{20}$.

So, similarly,

$X = \dfrac{1}{3} + \dfrac{1}{2} = \dfrac{2+3}{6} = \dfrac{5}{6}$

$Y = \dfrac{5}{6} + \dfrac{3}{4} = \dfrac{10+9}{12} = \dfrac{19}{12}$

and $Z = \dfrac{19}{12} + 1\dfrac{1}{5} = 2\dfrac{47}{60}$

30. (C)   31. (C)   32. (A)   33. (B)

34. (C) $\dfrac{2}{3}$ of a number is smaller than thrice the same number by 49.

So, 3(Number) $- \dfrac{2}{3}$ (Number) = 49

$= \left(3 - \dfrac{2}{3}\right)$ (Number) = 49

$= \left(\dfrac{9-2}{3}\right)$ (Number) = 49

$\therefore$ Number $= \overset{7}{\cancel{49}} \times \dfrac{3}{\cancel{7}} = 21$

35. (A) Fraction of cloth left $= 1 - \dfrac{2}{5} = \dfrac{3}{5}$

$\therefore$ Length of the cloth left

$= \dfrac{3}{5} \times \dfrac{7}{8}$ m $= \dfrac{21}{40}$ m

36. (C) $\dfrac{3}{4}, 1\dfrac{4}{5}, 2\dfrac{5}{6}, \boxed{?}, 4\dfrac{7}{8}$

$= \dfrac{3}{4}, \dfrac{9}{5}, \dfrac{17}{6}, \boxed{}, \dfrac{39}{8}$

with $+6, +8, +10, +12$ over numerators and $+1, +1, +1, +1$ under denominators

$\therefore$ The missing fraction

$= \dfrac{17+10}{6+1} = \dfrac{27}{7} = 3\dfrac{6}{7}$

37. (D) The required fraction $= \dfrac{55 \text{ minutes}}{2\dfrac{1}{4} \text{ hours}}$

$= \dfrac{55}{\dfrac{9}{4} \times 60} = \dfrac{55 \times 4}{9 \times 60} = \dfrac{11}{27}$

38. (B) The required fraction

$$= \frac{6}{7} \text{ kg} \div 12$$

$$= \left(\frac{6}{7} \times \frac{1}{12}\right) \text{kg} = \frac{1}{14} \text{ kg}$$

39. (A) $\frac{14}{15} \div 6 = \frac{14}{15} \times \frac{1}{6}$

$$= \frac{7}{15 \times 3} = \frac{7}{45}$$

40. (C) Quantity of salt sold $= 4\frac{4}{5}$ kg

Quantity of salt left $= 4\frac{7}{10}$ kg

∴ Quantity of salt in the shop at first

$$= 4\frac{4}{5} + 4\frac{7}{10} = 9\frac{1}{2} \text{ kg}$$

41. (C)   42. (C)   43. (D)

☞ **Previous Contest Questions**

1. (A) Capacity of a jar $= 6\,l = 8$ mugs

∴ Capacity of a mug $= 6\,l \div 8$

$$= \frac{6}{8}\,l = \frac{3}{4}\,l$$

2. (B) Amount Manish had $= ₹\,45$

Fraction of the amount spent $= \frac{3}{5}$

∴ Amount left $= \left(1 - \frac{3}{5}\right) \times ₹\,45$

$$= \frac{2}{5} \times ₹\,45 = ₹\,18$$

3. (A) The required number

$$= 3\frac{3}{10} - 2\frac{2}{5} = \frac{9}{10}$$

4. (D) Height of Aarti

$$= \text{Height of Mona} + \frac{1}{4}\,m = 1\frac{5}{8}\,m$$

5. (B) Score of Pavan $= 76 = \frac{4}{5}$ of score of Prateek

$$\frac{4}{5} \rightarrow 76$$

$$\frac{5}{5} \rightarrow 76 \times \frac{5}{4}$$

$= 19 \times 5 = 95$

∴ Their total marks $= 76 + 95 = 171$

6. (C) Volume of water in the tank

$$= \frac{4}{5} \times 32\,l$$

Volume of water poured into a pail

$$= \frac{1}{4} \text{ (Volume of water in the tank)}$$

Volume of water left in the tank

$$= \left(1 - \frac{1}{4}\right) \text{(Volume of water in the tank)}$$

$$= \frac{3}{4} \times \frac{4}{5} \times 32\,l = \frac{3 \times 32}{5}\,l$$

$$= \frac{96}{5}\,l = 19\frac{1}{5}\,l$$

7. (B)   8. (D)

9. (C) Numerator + Denominator = 67

After adding 31 to the denominator, the numerator is 3 units and denominator is 11 units.

3 + 11 = 14 units = 67 + 31 = 98

∴ 1 unit = 98 ÷ 14 = 7

3 units = 3 × 7 = 21 and

11 units = 11 × 7 = 77

New fraction $= \frac{21}{77}$

Hence, the original fraction

$$= \frac{21}{77 - 31} = \frac{21}{46}$$

10. (D) $\frac{5}{6} \times 15 = \frac{\boxed{?}}{12} \times 30$

On cancelling the factors common to numerator and denominator on both the sides,

$$\frac{5}{\underset{2}{6}} \times \cancel{15}^{5} = \frac{\square}{\underset{2}{\cancel{12}}} \times \cancel{30}^{5}$$

$$\frac{5 \times 5}{2} = \frac{\square}{2} \times 5$$

$$5 \times \frac{5}{2} = \square \times \frac{5}{2}$$

Hence the missing number is 5.

4. Decimals

☞ **Multiple Choice Questions**

1. (A) $\dfrac{78}{100} = 0.78$

2. (D) 3 tenths 5 thousandths

   $= \dfrac{3}{10} + \dfrac{5}{1000} = 0.305$

3. (D) $0.3 + 0.03 + 0.003 = 0.333$

4. (C) The required difference

   $= 32 - 27.091 = 4.909$

5. (B) $78.12 \times 1.5 = 117.18$

6. (A) $125.625 \div 0.5$

   $= \dfrac{125625}{1000} \div \dfrac{5}{10} = 251.25$

7. (B) 5 thousandths $= \dfrac{5}{1000} = 0.005$

8. (D) 2 tens 6 thousandths

   $= 20 + 0.006 = 20.006$

9. (D) When a decimal number is divided by 10, the decimal shifts left by 1 place.

   So, $9.826 \div 10 = 0.9826$

10. (D) $0.05 \times 0.09 \times 5 = 0.0225$

11. (C)
    ```
      18.0006
      14.005
    + 12.34
    ─────────
      44.3456
    ```

12. (D) As $2805 \div 2.55 = 1100$,

    $280.5 \div 25.5 = \dfrac{1100}{100} = 11$

13. (B) $0.23 = \dfrac{23}{100}$

14. (A) $\dfrac{0.1}{0.01} + \dfrac{0.01}{0.1} = 10 + \dfrac{1}{10} = 10 + 0.1$

    $= 10.1$

15. (B) $0.777 = 7 \times 0.111$

    $= 7 \times \dfrac{1}{9} = \dfrac{7}{9}$

16. (D) The cost of 15 pens = ₹ 148.50

    The cost of 1 pen = ₹ 148.50 ÷ 15
    = ₹ 9.90

17. (C) The cost of 1 litre of milk = ₹ 7.50

    ∴ The cost of 30.5 litres of milk
    = ₹ 7.50 × 30.5 = ₹ 228.75

18. (A)   19. (B)   20. (A)

21. (C) From the given decimal number line, the distance between two consecutive markings is $6.5 - 6.37 = 0.13$

    ∴ The value of P is $6.5 + 0.13 = 6.63$

    The value of Q is $6.63 + 0.13 = 6.76$

    The value of R is $6.76 + 0.13 = 6.89$

    ∴ $P + Q - R = 6.63 + 6.76 - 6.89$

    $= 6.50 = 6.5$

22. (A) 11.047 rounded to the nearest tenth is 11.0 as $4 < 5$.

23. (B) 32.4 rounded to the nearest ones is 32 as $4 < 5$ in the tenths place.

24. (C) $9.85 \approx 10$ and $23.099 \approx 23$

    ∴ $9.85 \times 23.099 \approx 10 \times 23$

25. (A) The difference of 5.47 and 5.07

    $= 5.47 - 5.07$

    $= 0.40 = 40$ hundredths

26. (D) 21 tenths = 2.1

    The difference of the given numbers
    $= 2.1 - 1.98 = 0.12 = 12$ hundredths

27. (B) $\dfrac{7}{8}$

    ```
         0.875
    8)7000
      -64
      ────
        60
       -56
       ────
        40
       -40
       ────
         0
    ```

    ∴ $\dfrac{7}{8} = 0.875 \approx 0.9$

28. (A) $14 + \dfrac{8}{10} + \dfrac{108}{100} + \dfrac{345}{1000}$

    $= 14 + 0.8 + 1.08 + 0.345 = 16.225$

29. (A) 65 hundredths = 0.65

    The required number is $130 \div 0.65$

    $= 130 \times \dfrac{100}{65} = 200$

30. (C) Quantity of water the tank can hold
= 20.145 l

Fraction of water used = $\dfrac{3}{5}$

∴ Quantity of water used

= $\dfrac{3}{5} \times (20.145)\, l = 12.087\, l$

31. (D) Quantity of water used = $\dfrac{3}{5} \times 20.145\, l$

∴ Quantity of water remaining in the tank

= $\left(1 - \dfrac{3}{5}\right) \times (20.145) l$

= $\dfrac{2}{5} \times 20.145\, l = 8.058\, l$

32. (D) The required product
= $39 \times (1.048 + 3.162)$
= $39 \times 4.210 = 164.19$

33. (B) Total length of the string = 18 m
Length of each equal part = 0.2 m

∴ No. of pieces = $\dfrac{18\ m}{0.2\ m} = \dfrac{180}{2} = 90$

34. (B) 0.19 > 0.11 > 0.109 > 0.10
So, 0.19 has the greatest value.

35. (D) Mass of grade I cashew nuts = 0.75 kg
Mass of grade II cashew nuts = 3.6 kg

∴ Total mass of cashew nuts

= (3.6 + 0.75) kg

= 4.35 kg

The mixture is packed equally into 5 packets.

∴ Mass of each packet

= $\dfrac{4.35}{5}$ kg = 0.87 kg

36. (B)   37. (C)   38. (A)

Previous Contest Questions

1. (B) The height of a wooden block
= 12.28 cm ≈ 12 cm

∴ The height of 14 similar blocks stacked on top = 12 × 14 = 168 cm

2. (D)   3. (C)   4. (B)

5. (A) 7.8 + 2.4 ÷ 60 − 0.09 = R

$7.8 + \left(\dfrac{2.4}{60}\right) - 0.09 = R$

$7.8 + \left(\dfrac{24}{600}\right) - 0.09 = R$

7.8 + 0.04 − 0.09 = R
7.84 − 0.09 = R
∴ R = 7.75
Rounding off R to 1 decimal place, we get 7.8.

6. (D) Actual : 14.36 × 23 = 330.28
Addition : 14.36 + 23 = 37.36
The difference between his answer and the actual answer
= 330.28 − 37.36 = 292.92

7. (A) 7 is the first digit of the decimal part of the given number.
So, 7 is in tenths place.

8. (B) 2 × 0.5 + 9 ÷ 0.3 + 10 × 0.92
= 1 + 30 + 9.2 = 40.2

9. (B) $\dfrac{17.28 \div 12}{3.6 \times 0.2} = \dfrac{17.28 \times \dfrac{1}{12}}{0.72}$

= $\dfrac{1728}{72 \times 12} = \dfrac{1728}{864} = 2$

10. (D) 0.3 ÷ 0.3 × 3 = 1 × 3 = 3

5. Arithmetic

Multiple Choice Questions

1. (A) 89% = $\dfrac{89}{100}$

2. (B) 79% = $\dfrac{79}{100} = 0.79$

3. (C) 0.97 = $\dfrac{97}{100} = 97\%$

4. (B) 75% of 35 kg
= $\dfrac{75}{100} \times 35$ kg = 26.25 kg

5. (C) 10% of ₹ 100 = ₹ 10
50% of ₹ 10 = ₹ 5
Since ₹ 10 > ₹ 5, 10% of ₹ 100 > 50% of ₹ 10.

6. (B) Total number of plants in the garden = 400

Percentage of jasmine plants = 100% – Sum of % different coloured of rose plants

= 100% – (10 + 30 + 40)%

= 100% – 80% = 20%

Thus, 20% of 400 plants are jasmine plants.

The number of jasmine plants

= 20% × 400 = 80

7. (C) Total marks = 450

Marks scored = 312

∴ % of marks scored

$= \dfrac{312}{450} \times 100\% = 69.33\%$

8. (D) 6 squares out of 32 are coloured.

∴ The required percentage

$= \dfrac{6}{32} \times 100\% = 18.75\%$

9. (C) Amount given by Rohan's mother = ₹ 300

% of money spent on stationery and eatables

= 15% + 35% = 50%

The % of amount saved

= Remaining % = (100 – 50)% = 50%

∴ Amount saved by Rohan

= 50% of ₹ 300

$= \dfrac{50}{100} \times ₹ 300 = ₹ 150$

10. (A) A chess board has 8 × 8 = 64 squares of which 32 are black.

Hence, the percentage of black squares

$= \dfrac{32}{64} \times 100\% = 50\%.$

11. (A) Percentage of maths teachers

$= \dfrac{\text{No. of maths teachers}}{\text{Total no. of teachers}} \times 100\%$

$= \dfrac{15}{125} \times 100\% = 12\%$

12. (B) Cash remaining with Prashanth

= [100% – (65 + 20)%] of total investment

= 15% of total investment

∴ ₹ 1305 $= \dfrac{15}{100} \times$ total investment

Hence, the total investment

$= ₹ 1305 \times \dfrac{100}{15} = ₹ 8700$

13. (C) 37.5% of a number = 450

$\dfrac{37.5}{100} \times \text{Number} = 450$

∴ Number $= \dfrac{450 \times 100}{37.5} = 1200$

∴ 87.5% of the same number

$= \dfrac{87.5}{100} \times 1200$

= 87.5 × 12 = 1050

14. (A) The required percentage

$= \dfrac{108}{270} \times 100\% = 40\%$

15. (C) Let the third number be 100.

Required % $= \dfrac{120 \times 100}{150} = 80\%$

16. (D) Increased salary of the man

= 120% of his salary before increase

∴ His salary before increase

= Increased salary $\times \dfrac{100}{120}$

$= ₹ 3000 \times \dfrac{100}{120} = ₹ 2500$

17. (B) Average $= \dfrac{66 + 14 + 16}{8}$ years

= 12 years

18. (A) 28.5 × 7 – 27 × 3 – 29 × 3 = 31.5 °C

19. (D) $\dfrac{5 + 0 + 6 + \dfrac{1}{4} + 8\dfrac{3}{4}}{5} = \dfrac{20}{5} = 4$

20. (B) The required ratio is

₹ 3 : 60 p

= 300 p : 60 p (Since ₹ 1 = 100 p)

= 5 : 1

21. (C) 50 : 30 = 5 : 3

22. (C) 0.12 kg : 180 g

= 120 g : 180 g = 2 : 3

23. (B) $60 \times \dfrac{2}{5} = ₹ 24$

$60 \times \dfrac{3}{5} = ₹ 36$

Difference = ₹(36 – 24) = ₹ 12

24. (A) Total marks = 75 + 25 = 100
Required ratio = 75 : 100 = 3 : 4

25. (C) Height of A = $\dfrac{4}{3} \times$ Height of B

$= \dfrac{4}{3} \times 1.2$ m $= 1.6$ m

26. (B) Speed $= \dfrac{\text{Distance}}{\text{Time}} = \dfrac{150 \text{ km}}{5 \text{ h}}$

$= 30$ km/hr

27. (C) Distance = 800 m
Time = 15 min = 15 × 60 seconds

Speed $= \dfrac{800}{15 \times 60} = \dfrac{8}{9}$ m/s

28. (B) Time $= \dfrac{\text{Distance}}{\text{Speed}} = \dfrac{90}{45} = 2$ hours

29. (A) Speed = 45 km/h

Time = 36 minutes $= \dfrac{36}{60}$ hr

Distance = Speed × Time

$= 45 \times \dfrac{36}{60} = 27$ km

30. (B) Distance = 1 km = 1000 m
Speed = 8 m/s

Time $= \dfrac{\text{Distance}}{\text{Speed}}$

$= \dfrac{1000}{8} = 125$ sec

31. (B) Amount (A) = ₹ 450
Principal (P) = ₹ 415
I = A − P = ₹ (450 − 415) = ₹ 35

32. (B) P = A − I   = ₹ (500 − 100)
= ₹ 400

33. (A) P = ₹ 1800, A = ₹ 2700,
T = 10 years
I = A − P = ₹ (2700 − 1800) = ₹ 900

R $= \dfrac{100 \times I}{P \times T} = \dfrac{100 \times 900}{1800 \times 10} = 5\%$

34. (C) No. of questions in Manu's test = 100
No. of questions she completed = 40
∴ Percentage of questions completed

$= \dfrac{40}{100} \times 100\% = 40\%$

35. (C) Gain = S.P. − C.P. = ₹ (10 − 5) = ₹ 5

$= \dfrac{\text{Gain}}{\text{C.P}} \times 100\%$

$= \dfrac{5}{5} \times 100\% = 100\%$

36. (A) Average $= \dfrac{\text{Total marks}}{\text{Number of tests}}$

$\Rightarrow 70 = \dfrac{\text{Total marks}}{5}$

∴ Total marks = 350

37. (A) The required ratio
= (No. of   :   (Total no.
red marbles)   of marbles)
= 9 : (15 + 9)
= 9 : 24 = 3 : 8

38. (C) The required ratio =
= (No. of   :   (Total no.
blue marbles)   of marbles)
= 15 : (15 + 9)
= 15 : 24 = 5 : 8

39. (A) No. of blue marbles = 15
Total number of marbles = 24
∴ Percentage of blue marbles

$= \dfrac{15}{24} \times 100\% = 62\dfrac{1}{2}\%$

40. (B) Percentage of red marbles

$= \dfrac{\text{No. of marbles}}{\text{Total no. of marbles}} \times 100\%$

$= \dfrac{9}{24} \times 100\% = 37\dfrac{1}{2}\%$

The required decimal equivalent = 37.5%

$= \dfrac{37.5}{100} = 0.375$

41. (D) 30% of a number = 24

$1\dfrac{1}{2}$ times a number

= 150% of the number

$= \dfrac{24}{30} \times 150 = 120$

42. (C) 25% of $50 = \dfrac{25}{100} \times 50 = 12.5$

250% of $20 = \dfrac{250}{100} \times 20 = 50$

$\therefore$ The required difference
$= 50 - 12.5 = 37.5$

43. (D) $1\dfrac{1}{3}$ h $= 60$ min $+ \dfrac{1}{3} \times 60$ min

$= (60 + 20)$ min $= 80$ min

15% of $1\dfrac{1}{3}$ h $= 15\%$ of 80 min

$= \dfrac{15}{100} \times 80$ min $= 12$ min

44. (A) The average of X and Y $= 108$

$\Rightarrow$ X + Y $= 108 \times 2 = 216 \rightarrow (1)$

300% X = Y i.e., Y = 3X

X + Y = 216

$\Rightarrow$ X + 3X = 216

$\Rightarrow$ 4X = 216

$\Rightarrow$ X $= \dfrac{216}{4} = 54$

The required difference
$= Y - X = 3X - X$

$= 2X = 2 \times 54 = 108$

45. (B) No. of girls $= 42 - 12 = 30$

$\therefore$ The ratio of number of girls to no. of boys $= 30 : 12 = 5 : 2$.

46. (B) $\boxed{} : 3 = 12 : 36$

$= 1 : 3$

$\therefore$ The missing number is 1.

47. (C) Average $=$

$\dfrac{\text{Sum of quantities}}{\text{Number of quantities}}$

Sum of the quantities

$=$ Average $\times$ No. of quantities

$= 12 \times 6 = 72$

48. (D)   49. (A)   50. (D)   51. (B)

☞ **Previous Contest Questions**

1. (D) Amount left with Madhu

$= (100 - 25)\%$ of ₹ 248

$= 75\%$ of ₹ 248 $=$ ₹ 186

2. (C) Earnings of Mrs. Kumar

$=$ ₹$(1000 - 250) =$ ₹ 750

$\therefore$ Ratio $= 1000 : 750 = 4 : 3$

3. (A) 20% of 3 kg 400 g

$= \dfrac{20}{100} \times 3400$ g $= 680$ g

4. (B) Number of pages read in that hour
$= 30\%$ of 90

$= \dfrac{30}{100} \times 90 = 27$

5. (C) 28% of 1050 pupils can swim

$\therefore$ No. of pupils who cannot swim
$= (100 - 28)\%$ of 1050

$= \dfrac{72}{100} \times 1050 = 756$

6. (B) No. of squares shaded $= 6$

Total number of squares $= 18$

$\therefore$ Their ratio $= 6 : 18 = 1 : 3$

7. (D) P + Q $= 105$

P $-$ Q $= 45$

So, 2P $= 105 + 45 = 150$

$\Rightarrow$ P $= 75$

Then, Q $=$ P $- 45 = 75 - 45 = 30$

$\therefore$ P : Q $= 75 : 30 = 5 : 2$

8. (C) $0.1\% = \dfrac{0.1}{100} = \dfrac{1}{1000}$

9. (A) No. of questions $= 50$

No. of correct answers $= 38$

No. of incorrect answers $= 12$

$\therefore$ The required percentage of questions answered incorrectly

$= \dfrac{12}{50} \times 100\% = 24\%$

10. (B) The average mass of the given blocks

$= \dfrac{59 + 67 + 44 + 54 + 28}{5}$ kg

$= \dfrac{252}{5} = 50.4$ kg

6. Geometry

☞ **Multiple Choice Questions**

1. (C)   2. (B)   3. (D)   4. (D)   5. (B)

6. (A)   7. (C)   8. (B)   9. (D)   10. (C)

11. (D)

12. (B)   A right angle is formed between the hands of a clock at 3 O'clock.

13. (A)   An acute angle is formed between the hands of a clock at 5: 20 p.m.

14. (A)   15. (B)   16. (D)   17. (B)   18. (C)

19. (A)   20. (C)   21. (B)   22. (A)   23. (B)

24. (C)   25. (D)   26. (A)   27. (A)   28. (D)

29. (D)   30. (B)   31. (D)   32. (A)   33. (C)

34. (B)   35. (D)   36. (B)

37. (A)

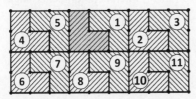

∴ 11 more such basic shapes fill up the given box.

38. (D)   The unit shape in the given tessellation is △.

39. (C) $\angle a + \angle b + \angle c = 180°$

∴ $\angle a = 180° - 62° - 77°$

= $180° - 139° = 41°$

40. (D) $\frac{5}{6}$ of a complete turn

= $\frac{5}{6} \times 360° = 5 \times 60° = 300°$

41. (A) $\angle a + 90° = 155°$

∴ $\angle a = 65°$

42. (C) $\angle p + \angle q + 58° + 90° = 360°$

$3 \angle q + \angle q + 148° = 360°$

$4 \angle q = 360° - 148° = 212°$

∴ $\angle q = \frac{212°}{4} = 53°$

$\angle p = 3 \angle q = 3 \times 53° = 159°$

43. (A) $\angle x = \angle y = \angle z = \frac{90°}{3} = 30°$

$\angle w + \angle x = 90° + 30° = 120°$

44. (D)   Chord MN and QR pass through the centre O of the circle. So, they are diameters.

45. (D)   The angle 'm' given lies between 180° and 270°. An estimate of the answer = 250° as an exact 90°

46. (C)

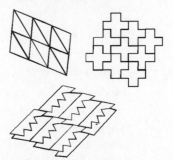

47. (B) $\angle COB = \angle AOD = 70° = \angle x + \angle y$

$\angle x : \angle y = 3 : 2$

∴ 5 units = 70°

Thus, 1 unit = $\frac{70°}{5} = 14°$

$\angle x = 3$ units = $3 \times 14° = 42°$

48. (C) $\angle x + \angle v = 2 \angle x = 2 \angle v$ but not 180°.

49. (A)   50. (A)

☞ **Previous Contest Questions**

1. (B)   After 10 hours, the time would be 2 o'clock.

In 12 hours, the hour hand moves through 360°.

∴ For 10 hours, the hour hand moves through $\frac{360°}{12} \times 10 = 300°$

2. (B) $\angle DOQ = \angle COP = 60°$

$\angle y = 60°$

$\angle x = \dfrac{2}{3} \times 60° = 40°$

$\angle z = 180° - 60° - 40° = 80°$

$\dfrac{\angle x}{\angle z} = \dfrac{40°}{80°} = \dfrac{1}{2}$

3. (B) $\angle WUZ = \angle YUX = 28°$

4. (B) $\angle AOB = \angle DOC$

$\Rightarrow \angle AOB = \dfrac{180° - 88°}{2} = 46°$

$\angle p = \angle AOB = 46°$

5. (C) $x° + 4x° = 90°$

$\Rightarrow x° = \dfrac{90°}{5} = 18°$

6. (C) $3y + 2y = 180°$

$\Rightarrow y = 180° \div 5 = 36°$

$x = 2y = 2 \times 36° = 72°$

7. (A) Given, $\angle w : \angle x : \angle y : \angle z = 1 : 3 : 5 : 6$

$1 + 3 + 5 + 6 = 15$ units

15 units $= 360°$

1 unit $= 360° \div 15 = 24°$

3 units $= 3 \times 24° = 72°$

5 units $= 5 \times 24° = 120°$

6 units $= 6 \times 24° = 144°$

8. (B) The sum of the three angles in a triangle is 180°.

$\angle BAC = 180° - (90° + 21°) = 69°$

9. (A) In a quadrilateral, the sum of all the angles is 360°.

So, $\angle g = 360° - 138° - 90° - 90°$

$= 360° - 318° = 42°$

7. Mensuration

👉 **Multiple Choice Questions**

1. (C)   2. (D)   3. (D)

4. (B)   5. (A)   6. (B)

7. (C) Area of a square of side 13 m is

13×13 sq m $= 169$ sq m

8. (C) Area of a rectangle of length 13 m and width 12 m

$= 13 \times 12$ sq m $= 156$ sq m

9. (B) Length (l), Breadth (b)

$\Rightarrow P = 2(l + b)$ units

When length and breadth are doubled,

$l \rightarrow 2l \qquad b \rightarrow 2b$

Then $P = 2(2l + 2b)$

$= 2 \times [2(l + b)] = 2 \times P$

i.e., perimeter is doubled.

10. (B) Length $= \dfrac{\text{Area}}{\text{breadth}} = \dfrac{120 \text{ sq m}}{5 \text{ m}} = 24$ m

11. (C) The area of a square $= 144$ sq m

i.e., side $\times$ side $= 144$ sq m

$= (12 \times 12)$ sq m

$\therefore$ The side of the square $= 12$ m

12. (A)

Length of the rectangle $= 32$ m

It is partitioned into two equal square rooms. So, side of the square room

$= \dfrac{1}{2} \times 32 \text{ m} = 16 \text{ m}$ = The length of

the partition.

13. (A) Perimeter of the rectangle $= 132$ m

$= 2(l + b) = 132$ m

$= 2\left(\dfrac{6b}{5} + b\right) = 132$ m

$\Rightarrow \dfrac{11b}{5} = 66$ m

$\Rightarrow b = \dfrac{66 \times 5}{11}$ m $= 30$ m

$\therefore l = \dfrac{6b}{5} = \dfrac{6 \times 30}{5} = 36$ m

Thus, area of the rectangle

$= l \times b = 36 \times 30 = 1080$ sq. m

14. (D)   15. (A)   16. (C)

17. (D) Volume of a cuboid $= l \times b \times h$

$= 10 \times 12 \times 8$ cu cm

$= 960$ cu cm

18. (D) A solid figure with 6 square faces is a cube.

19. (C) The volume of a cube of edge

$\dfrac{1}{4}$ cm $= \dfrac{1}{4 \times 4 \times 4}$ cu cm $= \dfrac{1}{64}$ cu cm

20. (A) Volume of the cube $= 25 \times 25 \times 25$ m^3
$= 15625$ m^3
Volume of the cuboid $= 20 \times 2 \times 3$
$= 120$ m^3
∴ Volume of cube > Volume of cuboid.

21. (A) P $= 12 \times 12 \times 12$ m$^3 = 1728$ cu m
Q $= 8 \times 6 \times 4$ m$^3 = 192$ cu m
Clearly, P is greater than Q.

22. (A) Dimensions of a box
$= 9$ cm $\times 3.5$ cm $\times 7.5$ cm
Capacity of the box $= 9 \times 3.5 \times 7.5$ cu cm
$= 236.25$ cu cm

23. (D) Volume of cuboid $= 10$ cm $\times 2.5$ cm $\times 5$ cm
$= 50 \times 2.5 = 125$ cm^3
Volume of cuboid = Volume of a cube
∴ The measure of edge of the cube
$= 5$ cm

24. (A) The shaded area of two faces of the cube $= 72$ m^2
∴ The shaded area of one face
$= \dfrac{72}{2}$ m$^2 = 36$ m^2
$\Rightarrow$ side or edge of the cube $= 6$ m
Hence, its volume $= 6 \times 6 \times 6$ cu m
$= 216$ cu m

25. (C) 26. (C) 27. (B)

28. (D) Volume of water in the tank
$= $ Volume of the tank
$= 15 \times 12 \times 8$ cm^3
$= 1440$ cm^3

29. (C) Capacity of the tank
$= 20 \times 30 \times 45$ cm^3
$= 27000$ cm^3
$= 27\,l$ (Since 1000 cm$^3 = 1\,l$)

30. (A) 31. (D)

32. (A) Area of square formed $= 49$ cm^2
So, its side $= 7$ cm
Hence, the length of the wire
$= 4 \times 7$ cm $= 28$ cm

33. (C) Total volume of water in the tank
$= 2250$ cm$^3 + 6430$ cm$^3 = 8680$ cm^3
1000 cm$^3 = 1\,l$
∴ 8680 cm$^3 = \dfrac{8680}{1000}\,l = 8.68\,l$

34. (D) Volume of 4 similar cubes of side
5 cm $= 4 \times 5 \times 5 \times 5$ cm$^3 = 500$ cm^3

35. (D) The perimeter of the given net
$= 12 \times 4$ cm $= 48$ cm

36. (A) The area of the cardboard needed to make the net $= (4 \times 4) \times 5$ cm$^2 = 80$ cm^2

37. (B) Volume of the cube
$= $ Area of the base $\times$ height
$= (4 \times 4)$ cm$^2 \times 4$ cm $= 64$ cm^3

38. (B) 39. (D)

40. (D) Volume the given solid = Total volume of the three solids in it.
$= [(2 \times 2 \times 3) + (7 \times 3 \times 5) + (5 \times 3 \times 3)]$ cm^3
$= [12 + 105 + 45]$ cm$^3 = 162$ cm^3

41. (A) Perimeter of square X is 20 cm. So, its
side $= \dfrac{20}{4}$ cm $= 5$ cm
Perimeter of square Y is 36 cm. So, its
side $= \dfrac{36}{4}$ cm $= 9$ cm
Hence, their difference $= (9 - 5)$ cm
$= 4$ cm

42. (B) The total area of X and Y is
$[(5 \times 5) + (9 \times 9)]$ cm^2
$= (25 + 81)$ cm$^2 = 106$ cm^2

43. (D) The given figure can be re-aligned as shown for easier computation of the number of sides.

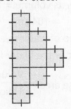

∴ No. of sides $= 16$
Length of each side $= 3$ cm
∴ Perimeter of the given figure
$= 16 \times 3$ cm $= 48$ cm

44. (B) Area of square $= 144$ cm^2
∴ Its side $= 12$ cm
Hence, the required perimeter
$= 5 \times 12$ cm $= 60$ cm

45. (C) According to the given problem,
PR $= $ RQ $= 1.5 \times 4.8$ m $= 7.2$ m
Perimeter of $\triangle$ PQR $= (2 \times 7.2 + 4.8)$ m
$= 19.2$ m

Explanatory Answers

Ratio of perimeter of the square and the triangle = 4 : 3

Perimeter of square = $\dfrac{19.2}{3} \times 4$ = 25.6 m

∴ Side of the square = $\dfrac{25.6}{4}$ m = 6.4 m

Hence, area of the square = 6.4×6.4 m^2
$= 40.96$ m^2

☞ Previous Contest Questions

1. (B)   Perimeter = 18 units

8 units

Given perimeter = 61.2 m

18 units = 61.2 m

1 unit = $\dfrac{61.2}{18}$ m = 3.4 m

Difference between length and breadth = 7 units
$= 7 \times 3.4$ m
$= 23.8$ m
$= 2380$ cm

2. (A)   The given figure becomes a cuboid if it has $4 \times 3 \times 2 = 24$ cubes.

The no. of cubes in the given figure = 11

∴ The no. of cubes that must be added to make it a cuboid = 24 – 11 = 13

Hence, its volume = $13 \times 2 \times 2 \times 2$ cm^3
$= 104$ cm^3

3. (C)   Volume of water in a tank = 625 cm^3

Height of the water level = 5 cm

∴ Base area = $\dfrac{\text{Volume}}{\text{Height}}$

$= \dfrac{625 \text{ cm}^3}{5 \text{ cm}} = 125$ cm^2

4. (D)   Perimeter = 10 units

Ratio of perimeter and length = 10 : 3

3 units

P = 10 units

3 units

∴ Breadth = $\dfrac{10 - 2 \times 3}{2}$

2 units → 8 cm (Given)

---

1 unit → 4 cm

3 units → 4 cm × 3 = 12 cm = length

Area → 12 cm × 8 cm = 96 cm^2

5. (B)   Perimeter of rectangle = 28 cm
$= 2(8 + b)$ cm

∴ $b = \left(\dfrac{28}{2} - 8 \right)$ cm

$= (14 - 8)$ cm = 6 cm

Hence, the required ratio is 8 : 6 = 4 : 3

6. (A)   Ratio of length and breadth = 5 : 2

Area = $5 \times 2 = 10$ sq.units

Given area = 1690 cm^2

10 sq. units → 1690 cm^2

1 sq. unit → $\dfrac{1690}{10} = 169$ cm

1 unit = 13 cm

Perimeter = 2×7 units = 14 units

∴ Perimeter = $14 \times 13 = 182$ cm

7. (A)   Capacity of the container
$= 12 \times 10 \times 17$ cm^3
$= 2040$ cm^3

As it is half filled with rice, volume of rice in the container = $\dfrac{2040}{2}$ cm^3

$= 1020$ cm^3

8. (D)   Volume of each cube is
$3 \times 3 \times 3$ cm^3 = 27 cm^3

No. of cubes in the given $3 \times 2 \times 2 = 12$
∴ Volume of the cuboid = 12×27 cm^3
$= 324$ cm^3

9. (C)   Area of square = 64 cm^2

Side of square = 8 cm

Its perimeter = 4×8 cm = 32 cm

Perimeter of rectangle = $2(5 + l)$

$\dfrac{32}{2} - 5 = l \Rightarrow (16 - 5)$ cm = 11 cm

Area = $l \times b$

$= 11 \times 5 = 55$ cm^2

10. (D)   Ratio of sides of a triangle is 3 : 4 : 5

The longest side = 15 cm = 5 units

$\therefore$ 1 unit = $\dfrac{15}{5}$ cm = 3 cm

Hence, 3 units = 9 cm

and 4 units = 12 cm

Therefore, perimeter of the triangle

$\quad = (9 + 12 + 15)$ cm

$\quad = 36$ cm

8. Measurement

☞ **Multiple Choice Questions**

1. (A)   526.8 kg

$\quad\quad\quad \underline{- \ 287.93 \text{ kg}}$

$\quad\quad\quad \underline{ 238.87 \text{ kg}}$

$\quad\quad = 238$ kg 87 g

$\quad\quad \therefore$ P = 238 and Q = 87

2. (C)   18 months = 1 year 6 months

$\quad\quad \therefore$ 11 years 3 months + 1 year 6 months

$\quad\quad = 12$ years 9 months

So, Bhavani will be 12 years 9 months after 18 months' time from now.

3. (D)   Length of 5 pieces = $\dfrac{15}{8}$ m

Length of 1 piece = $\dfrac{15}{8}$ m $\div$ 5

$\quad\quad = \dfrac{15}{8} \times \dfrac{1}{5}$ m $= \dfrac{3}{8}$ m

$\quad\quad \therefore$ Length of original piece = Length of 12 pieces

$\quad\quad = \dfrac{3}{8}$ m $\times 12 = \dfrac{9}{2}$ m = 4.5 m

4. (B)   Boiling point of water on the Celsius scale is 100 °C.

5. (C)   3.6 l = 3.6 $\times$ 1000 ml = 3600 ml

73 l 80 ml

$\quad\quad = (73 \times 1000 + 80)$ ml = 73080 ml

$\quad\quad \therefore$ The required fraction = $\dfrac{3600}{73080}$

$\quad\quad = \dfrac{360}{7308} = \dfrac{10}{203}$

6. (D)   1 m 5 cm = 105 cm

3.5 km = 3.5 $\times$ 1000 m

$\quad = 3500$ m

$\quad = 3500 \times 100$ cm

$\quad = 350000$ cm

$\therefore$ The required ratio is

$105 : 350000 = 3 : 10000$

7. (B) $3\dfrac{1}{4}$ hours

$= (3 \times 60 + \dfrac{1}{4} \times 60)$ minutes

$= 195$ minutes.

No. of shirts altered in 39 minutes = 8

$\therefore$ No. of shirts that can be altered in

195 minutes = $\dfrac{8}{39} \times 195 = 40$

8. (A)   9. (D)   10. (A)   11. (D)   12. (B)

13. (A)   14. (A)

15. (C)   The Celsius scale is divided into 100 equal divisions each representing a degree.

16. (B)   2520 words $\rightarrow$ 1 h = 60 minutes

1680 words $\rightarrow \dfrac{60}{2520} \times 1680$ min

$= 40$ minutes

17. (C) $\dfrac{1}{4}$ tank $\rightarrow$ 16 l

$1 = \dfrac{4}{4}$ tank $\rightarrow 16\,l \times 4 = 64\,l$

18. (A)   Time at noon = 12

1 h 25 min before noon

$= 12 - 1$ h 25 min

$= 10$ h 35 min

$\therefore$ Rajesh left the office at 10 : 35 a.m.

19. (A)   Ratio of masses of Anita and Mamata = 4 : 7

Total units = 4 + 7 = 11

Total mass = 99 kg

$\therefore$ 1 unit = $\dfrac{99}{11}$ kg = 9 kg

Mamatas' mass = 7 units

$= 7 \times 9$ kg = 63 kg

20. (D)   Quantity of juice in each tin = 0.75 l

Total quantity in 5 tins

Explanatory Answers

$= 5 \times 0.15\,l = 3.75\,l$

Quantity of juice needed to fill up the 6 - litre container

$= 6\,l - 3.75\,l = 2.25\,l$

∴ No. of tins needed to be bought

$= \dfrac{2.25\,l}{0.75\,l} = 3$

21. **(A)** Temperature of Bat = 28 °C

≈ 30 °C (Rounded to the nearest ten.)

22. **(D)** Total mixture = 65 ml + 0.835 l
$= 0.065\,l + 0.835\,l = 0.900\,l = 0.9\,l$

Capacity of a cup = 0.09 l

∴ No. of cups needed $= \dfrac{0.9\,l}{0.09\,l} = 10$

23. **(B)** February 2013 has 28 days as 2013 is a non leapyear.

Wednesdays in the next weeks are 6th March (27 + 7), 13th March, 20th March and 27th March. So, 27th March 2013 was a Wednesday.

24. **(C)**   25. **(D)**

26. **(C)** The temperature indicated on the given thermometer is 37 °C, which is the normal body temperature of a human being.

27. **(D)** Mass of a video recorder = 2400 g = 4 × mass of a camera

∴ Mass of a camera $= \dfrac{2400}{4}\,g = 600\,g$

$= 0.6\,kg$

28. **(A)** Parking fee per hour or part there of = ₹ 12.50

∴ Parking fee to be paid for $5\dfrac{1}{2}$ hours

$= ₹\ 12.50 \times 5\dfrac{1}{2}$

$= ₹\ 12.50 \times 5.5 = ₹\ 68.75$

29. **(D)** 40% of 6 m long cloth is used for flags and the remaining for skirts.

∴ Length of cloth used for skirts

= (100 – 40)% of 6 m

= 60% of 6 m

= 60% of 600 cm

$= \dfrac{60}{100} \times 600\ cm = 360\ cm$

Length of cloth needed for each skirt

= 1.2 m = 120 cm

∴ No. of skirts $= \dfrac{360\ cm}{120\ cm} = 3$

30. **(C)** No. of toys produced in 8 minutes = 720

∴ No. of toys produced in 6 minutes

$= \dfrac{720}{8} \times 6 = 540$

31. **(B)**

Amount of water in container A (in l)	Amount of water in container B (in l)	Amount of water in poured (in l)
15	5	0
16	6	1
17	7	2
18	8	3
19	9	4
20	10	5

The least amount of water poured into each container = 5 l = 5000 ml.

32. **(C)** 24 cups $\rightarrow \dfrac{3}{5}$ basin

$\dfrac{5}{5}$ basin $\rightarrow \dfrac{5}{3} \times 24 = 40$ cups

∴ To fill $\dfrac{1}{2}$ of the basin the no. of cups needed $= \dfrac{40}{2} = 20$

33. **(B)**   34. **(A)**   35. **(A)**   36. **(A)**

37. **(C)** Amount of water that flows into the tank in 1 min = 350 ml

$\dfrac{3}{4}$ hour $= \dfrac{3}{4} \times 60$ minutes = 45 minutes

1 min $\rightarrow$ 350 ml

45 min $\rightarrow$ 350 × 45 ml = 15.75 ml

38. **(B)** Mass of cashew nuts in the lighter box

$= \dfrac{2}{5} \times 20\ kg = 8\ kg = 8000\ g$

39. **(A)** 19 days before 30th April is 11th April as 11 + 19 = 30 (11th included.)

40. **(A)** Remaining juice

$= 3\,l - (0.196\,l + 200\ ml)$

$= 3000\ ml - (396\ ml)$

= 2604 ml

No. of bottles = 30

∴ Quantity of juice in each bottle

$= \dfrac{2604}{30} = 86.8$ ml

41. **(B)** Length of the rectangular field = 38 cm

Breadth = 24 cm

∴ Perimeter = 2(38 + 24)

$\qquad = 2 \times 62$ m

Flag poles are placed 2 m apart along the perimeter of the field.

∴ No. of flag poles around the field

$= \dfrac{2 \times 62 \text{ m}}{2 \text{ m}} = 62$

42. **(D)** 7 days = 1 week

∴ 1440 days $= \dfrac{1440}{7}$ weeks

= 205 weeks 5 days

43. **(D)** 8 kg 80 g = (8000 + 80) g

$\qquad = 8080$ g

$\qquad = 8.08$ kg

$\qquad \neq 8.008$ kg

44. **(B)** Mild weather is desirable to go on a picnic. The temperature range for mild weather is 20 °C – 25 °C.

45. **(C)** Total quantity of sugar = 600 kg

Quantity of sugar sold = 252 kg

Quantity of sugar remaining

= (600 – 252) kg = 348 kg

∴ Percentage of sugar remaining

$= \dfrac{348}{600} \times 100 \% = 58 \%$

👉 **Previous Contest Questions**

1. **(A)** Quantity of butter remaining

$= \left(\dfrac{5}{6} - \dfrac{1}{3} - \dfrac{1}{12} \right) \text{ kg} = \dfrac{5}{12} \text{ kg}$

$= \dfrac{5}{12} \times 1000 \text{ g} = 416.66 \text{ g} \approx 417 \text{ g}$

2. **(B)** Initial temperature on Sunday = 34 °C

Total fall in temperature by 2: 00 a.m. on Monday

= 9 °C + 3 °C = 12 °C

The temperature at 2: 00 a.m. On Monday = 34 °C – 12 °C = 22 °C

The temperature rose by 8 °C by 8: 00 a.m. on Monday.

∴ Final temperature at 8: 00 a.m. on Monday. = 22 °C + 8 °C = 30 °C

3. **(D)** Age difference between Sunitha and her son = (65 – 36) years = 29 years.

So, 7 years ago, Sunitha's age was twice her son's age.

4. **(B)** From the figure, the 5th mark denotes the height of pole P which is 225 cm.

So, each marking is at $\dfrac{225}{5}$ cm = 45 cm

Pole Q is at the 4th mark. So, the height of pole Q = 4 × 45 cm = 180 cm

The difference = 3 m – 180 cm

= (300 – 180) cm = 120 cm

So, pole Q is 120 cm less than 3m.

5. **(A)** Temperature of the rod = 120 °C

Amount of heat lost every minute = 2 °C

∴ Amount of heat lost for 16 minutes = 16 × 2 °C = 32 °C

∴ The temperature of the rod after 16 minutes

= 120 °C – 32 °C = 88 °C

6. **(D)**   7. **(C)**

8. **(B)** Average height of children = 84 cm

∴ Their total height

= 3 × 84 cm = 252 cm

Height of Bhaskar

= [252 – (78 + 90)] cm

= (252 – 168) cm = 84 cm

9. **(C)** Water boils at 100 °C.

∴ The temperature that is to be increased = (100 – 38.5) °C = 61.5 °C

10. **(A)** 1 min → 250 ml

12 min → 12 × 250 ml = 3 l

11. **(D)** 250 ml → 1 min

8 l = 8000 ml → $\dfrac{8000}{250}$ min = 32 min

12. **(C)** Numbers that can be rounded as 17000 to the nearest thousand are 16500 to 17499. Hence the greatest mass of the basket of fruits could be 17499 g.

9. Data Handling

☞ **Multiple Choice Questions**

1. (A) No. of secondary school students
$= 500 = 2 \times 250$

$= 2 \times$ No. of tertiary students.

2. (D) The no. of primary school students $= 350$

$\dfrac{1}{5}$ of 350 are below 10 years old.

So, $\dfrac{4}{5}$ of 350 are 10 years old and above.

∴ The required number $= \dfrac{4}{5} \times 350$

$= 280$

3. (B) Mass of the heaviest child $= 35$ kg

Mass of the lightest child $= 20$ kg

Their difference $= 15$ kg

4. (C) From the graph, the two bars corresponding to the mass of Roja and Swapna are of the same height. So, Roja and Swapna have the same mass.

5. (A) Mass of Swathi $= 20$ kg

15 kg heavier than Swathi

$= 20$ kg $+ 15$ kg

$= 35$ kg

$=$ Mass of Tarun

6. (C) $\dfrac{3}{4}$ of Beena's marks

$= \dfrac{3}{4} \times 80 = 60 =$ Marks scored by Shruthi

7. (C) 8. (A)

9. (A) Amount saved in January $= ₹ 1200$

The percent of his salary saved

$= \dfrac{₹ 1200}{₹ 2500} \times 100\% = 48\%$

∴ The percent of money spent
$= (100 - 48)\% = 52\%$

10. (B) Amount saved in February $= ₹ 1500$

Amount spent

$= ₹ 2500 - ₹ 1500 = ₹ 1000$

Twice the amount spent in February
$= 2 \times ₹ 1000 = ₹ 2000$

∴ Saving in that month

$= ₹ 2500 - ₹ 2000 = ₹ 500$

$=$ Saving in March

11. (A) 12. (B) 13. (D) 14. (A) 15. (B)

16. (D) Amount earned on Monday $= ₹ 80$

∴ ₹ 100 more than ₹ 80 is ₹ 180
$=$ Amount earned on Friday

17.. (C) Average amount earned from Sunday to Wednesday

$= \dfrac{₹ (240 + 80 + 100 + 160)}{4}$

$= ₹ \dfrac{580}{4} = ₹ 145$

18. (A) Earnings on Tuesday $= ₹ 100$

$\dfrac{4}{5}$ of ₹ 100 $= ₹ 80$

$=$ Amount earned on Monday

19. (B) Amount earned on Friday $= ₹ 180$

$= ₹ 80 + ₹ 100$

$=$ Amount earned on Monday and Tuesday

20. (C) Amount earned on weekdays

$= ₹ (80 + 100 + 160 + 140 + 180)$

$= ₹ 660$

Amount earned on weekends

$= ₹ (220 + 240) = ₹ 460$

∴ The required ratio

$= 660 : 460$

$= 33 : 23$

21. (B) Average time taken by the boys

$= \dfrac{63 + 60 + 66 + 59 + 68}{5}$

$= \dfrac{316}{5} = 63.2$ seconds

22. (C) 23. (D)

24. (B) Maya's savings $= \dfrac{2}{5}$ of her allowance

50% of savings is deposited in the bank.

Amount deposited in the bank

$= \left(\dfrac{2}{5} \times \dfrac{50}{100} \times \text{allowance} \right)$

$= \dfrac{1}{5} \times$ allowance

$= ₹ 120$ (Given)

∴ Allowance $= ₹ 120 \times 5 = ₹ 600$

25. (A) Since AB is the diameter, and 12% is spent on stationery, $(50 - 12)\%$

= 38% is spent on food and transport in the ratio 9 : 10.

∴ Percentage amount spent on transport per month is $\dfrac{10}{19} \times 38\%$

= 20%

Hence, amount spent on transport per month

$= \dfrac{20}{100} \times ₹\,600 = ₹\,120$

Thus, amount spent on transport per year

$= 12 \times ₹\,120 = ₹\,1440$

26. (C)   Part of the pie-chart representing students who like apple is 25%.

25% → 10 students

$15\% \to \dfrac{10}{25} \times 15 = 6$ students

27. (D)   28. (C)   29. (B)

30. (A)   The number of pupils who failed = 4

The number of pupils who passed = 40 – 4 = 36

∴ The required ratio = 36 : 4 = 9 : 1

31. (D)   The number of pupils who secured the Honors grade = 8 + 7 = 15

The required percentage

$= \dfrac{15}{40} \times 100\% = 37.5\%$

32. (A)   33. (D)   34. (C)   35. (D)

36. (A)   Percentage of sunflowers sold = 44%

Percentage of lilies sold = 13%

Their difference = (44 – 13)% = 31%

∴ The required percent

$= \dfrac{31}{13} \times 100\% = 238\dfrac{6}{13}\%$

37. (C)   Fraction representing blue T-shirts

$= 1 - \left(\dfrac{1}{5} + \dfrac{2}{5} + \dfrac{1}{4} \right)$

$= 1 - \dfrac{17}{20} = \dfrac{3}{20}$

$\dfrac{2}{5} \to 1400$ means $\dfrac{8}{20} \to 1400$

$\dfrac{3}{20} \to 1400 \times \dfrac{20}{8} \times \dfrac{3}{20} = 525$

∴ No. of blue T-shirts sold = 525

38. (D)   Percentage of Bananas $= \dfrac{3}{5} \times 100\% = 60\%$

∴ Percentage of watermelons
= (100 – 60 – 15.1 – 13.5)%
= (100 – 88.6)% = 11.4%

39. (A)   The fraction representing the number of lorries $= \dfrac{3}{25}$

Total number of vehicles = 7000

∴ Number of lorries $= \dfrac{3}{25} \times 7000$

= 840

40. (C)   The fraction representing the 'Others' in the pie-chart

$= 1 - \left(\dfrac{1}{4} + \dfrac{19}{50} + \dfrac{3}{25} + \dfrac{9}{50} \right) = \dfrac{7}{100}$

Given 30% of the 'Others' are cycles, the number of cycles = 30% of $\dfrac{7}{100}$ of 7000

$= \dfrac{30}{100} \times \dfrac{7}{100} \times 7000 = 147$

41. (B)   42. (A)   43. (A)   44. (D)

45. (B)   No. of students who answered question 1 correctly = 2

No. of students who answered question 4 correctly = 5

Their difference = 5 – 2 = 3

46. (C)   47. (B)   48. (B)   49. (B)

50. (A)   The average amount of money saved by Sonu in the given week

$= \dfrac{₹\,(0 + 4 + 8 + 9 + 9 + 12 + 14)}{7}$

$= \dfrac{₹\,56}{7} = ₹\,8$

☞ **Previous Contest Questions**

1. (C)   Increase in the number of visitors on Tuesday and Wednesday = 1200 – 750

= 450

∴ The required percentage

$= \dfrac{450}{750} \times 100\% = 60\%$

2.   (B)   The total number of visitors on the given 5 days = 500 + 750 + 1200 + 900 + 1250 = 4600

3.   (D)   The average number of visitors to the science fair per day

$$= \frac{500 + 750 + 1200 + 900 + 1250}{5}$$

= 920 ≈ 900 (Rounded to the nearest hundred.)

4.   (A)   The marking for 3rd week is at 6.

Therefore, the amount of money collected in the 3rd week

= 6 × ₹ 1000 = ₹ 6000

5.   (B)   6. (A)

7.   (C)   The total amount of money collected over 5 weeks = ₹ (4000 + 3000 + 6000 + 8000 + 12000) = ₹ 33000

∴ The required average

$$= \frac{33000}{5} = ₹ 6600$$

8.   (B)   9. (A)   10. (C)

Questions@stimulating-minds

1.   (C)   Each time Dev reaches into the jar, he removes half of the coins that are in the jar.

Since he removes half of the coins, then the other half of the coins remain in the jar.

We summarize Dev's progress in the table below.

Number of Times Coins are Removed	0	1	2	3	4	5	6
Number of Coins Remaining in the Jar	64	32	16	8	4	2	1

For exactly 1 coin to remain in the jar, Dev must reach in and remove coins from the jar 6 times.

2.   (C)   For every 3 chocolates that Simran buys at the regular price, she buys a fourth for ₹ 5.

Consider dividing the 12 chocolates that Simran buys into 3 groups of 4 chocolates.

In each group of 4, Simran buys 3 chocolates at the regular price and the fourth chocolate is purchased for ₹ 5.

That is, of the 12 chocolates that she buys, 3 are bought at ₹ 5 each while the remaining 9 are purchased at the regular price.

The total cost to purchase 3 chocolates at ₹ 5 each is 3 × ₹ 5 = ₹ 15.

Since Simran spent ₹ 105 and the total cost of the ₹ 5 chocolates was ₹ 15, then the cost of the regular price chocolates was ₹ 105 – ₹ 15 = ₹ 90.

Since 9 chocolate were purchased at the regular price for a total of ₹ 90, then the regular price of one chocolate

is $\frac{₹ \, 90}{9} = ₹ \, 10$

3.   (B)   The area of the rectangle is 8 × 4, or 32.

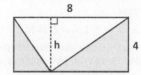

The unshaded portion of the rectangle is a triangle with base of length 8 and height h, as shown.

Since the dotted line (the height) with length h is parallel to the vertical side of the rectangle, then h = 4.

Thus, the area of the unshaded triangle

is $\frac{1}{2} × 8 × 4 = 4 × 4 = 16$.

The area of the shaded region is the area of the rectangle minus the area of the unshaded triangle.

Thus, the area of the shaded region is 32 – 16 = 16.

4.   (C)   If each of the four numbers is increased by 1, then the increase in their sum is 4.

That is, these four new numbers when added together have a sum that is 4 more than their previous sum T, or T + 4.

This new sum T + 4 is now tripled.

The result is 3 × (T + 4) = (T + 4) + (T + 4) + (T + 4) or 3T + 12.

5.   (B)   If 4 schools each recycle $\frac{3}{4}$ of a tonne of paper, then combined, they recycle

$4 × \frac{3}{4} = \frac{12}{4}$ = 3 tonnes of paper.

Since recycling 1 tonne of paper will save 24 trees, recycling 3 tonnes of paper will save 3 × 24 = 72 trees.

6.   (C)   Since the perimeter of the square is 48, its side length is $48 \div 4 = 12$.

Since the side length of the square is 12, its area is $12 \times 12 = 144$.

The area of the triangle is

$$\frac{1}{2} \times 48 \times x = 24x.$$

Since the area of the triangle equals the area of the square, then $24x = 144$ or $x = 6$.

7.   (D)   First, we try to figure out what digit Q is.

Since the product is not equal to 0, Q cannot be 0. Since the product has four digits and the top number has three digits, then Q (which is multiplying the top number) must be bigger than 1.

Looking at the units digits in the product, we see that $Q \times Q$ has a units digit of Q.

Since $Q > 1$, then Q must equal 5 or 6 (no other digit gives itself as a units digit when multiplied by itself).

But Q cannot be equal to 5, since if it was, the product RQ5Q would end "55" and each of the two parts (PPQ and Q) of the product would end with a 5. This would mean that each of the parts of the product was divisible by 5, so the product should be divisible by 5×5 = 25. But a number ending in 55 is not divisible by 25.

Therefore, $Q = 6$.

So the product now looks like

```
    P  P  6
×          6
————————————
    R  6  5  6
```

Now when we start the long multiplication, 6×6 gives 36, so we write down 6 and carry a 3.

When we multiply $P \times 6$ and add the carry of 3, we get a units digit of 5, so the units digit of $P \times 6$ should be 2.

For this to be the case, $P = 2$ or $P = 7$.

We can now try these possibilities: $226 \times 6 = 1356$ and $776 \times 6 = 4656$. Only

the second ends "656" like the product should.

So $P = 7$ and $R = 4$, and so $P + Q + R = 7 + 6 + 4 = 17$.

8.   (D)   To make a fraction as large as possible, we should make the numerator as large as possible and the denominator as small as possible.

Of the four numbers in the diagram, z is the largest and w is the smallest, so the largest possible fraction is $\frac{z}{w}$.

9.   (A)   We need to find two consecutive numbers the first of which is a multiple of 7 and the second of which is a multiple of 5.

We try the multiples of 7 and the numbers after each.

Do 7 and 8 work? No, since 8 is not a multiple of 5.

Do 14 and 15 work? Yes, since 15 is a multiple of 5.

This means that this year, Kriti is 15 years old.

So it will be 11 years until Kriti is 26 years old.

(Of course, Kriti could also be 50 years old or 85 years old this year, but then she would have already been 26 years old in the past.)

10.   (A)   Since the square has perimeter 24, then the side length of the square is

$$\frac{1}{4} \times 24 = 6.$$

Since the square has side length 6, then the area of the square is $6^2 = 36$.

Since the rectangle and the square have the same area, then the area of rectangle is 36.

Since the rectangle has area 36 and width 4, then the length of the rectangle is $\frac{36}{4} = 9$.

Since the rectangle has width 4 and length 9, then it has perimeter $4 + 9 + 4 + 9 = 26$.

Explanatory Answers

11. (A) In the diagram, B appears to be about 0.4 and C appears to be about 0.6, so B × C should be about 0.4 × 0.6 = 0.24.

Also, A appears to be about 0.2, so B × C is best represented by A.

12. (C) To maximize the number of songs used, Goutham should use as many of the shortest length songs as possible. (This is because he can always trade a longer song for a shorter songs and shorten the total time used).

If Goutham uses all 50 songs of 3 minutes in length, this takes 150 minutes.

There are 180 − 150 = 30 minutes left, so he can play an additional 30 ÷ 5 = 6 songs that are 5 minutes in length.

In total, he plays 50 + 6 = 56 songs.

13. (B) Suppose there are x balls in total in the bag.

Then there are $\frac{1}{3}x$ red balls and $\frac{2}{7}x$ blue balls.

This tells us that the number of green balls is $x - \frac{1}{3}x - \frac{2}{7}x = \frac{21}{21}x - \frac{7}{21}x - \frac{6}{21}x$

$= \frac{8}{21}x.$

But we know that the number of green balls is $2 \times \frac{2}{7}x - 8.$

Thus, $\frac{8}{21}x = 2 \times \left(\frac{2}{7}x\right) - 8$ or

$\frac{8}{21}x = \frac{12}{21}x - 8$ or $\frac{4}{21}x = 8$ or $x = 42.$

Since x = 42, the number of green balls is $\frac{8}{21}x = \frac{8}{21}(42) = 16.$

14. (B) From the given information, the total amount of marks obtained by the class is 20(80) + 8(90) + 2(100) = 2520.

Therefore, the class average is $\frac{2520}{30}$ = 84.

15. (C) Since the units digit of the product 39P × Q3 comes from multiplying P × 3, and this units digit is a 1, then P must be the digit 7.

Therefore, 397 × Q3 = 32 951 so Q3 $= \frac{32951}{397} = 83$, so Q = 8.

Thus, P + Q = 15.

16. (D) If 6 people each call 6 people in the first round of calls, there will be 36 people making 6 calls each for an additional 216 calls. Altogether, there will be the original 6, followed by 36 who in turn phone another 216.

In total, there are 6 + 36 + 216 = 258.

17. (C) Area of square = 4 × shaded part = 4 × 16 = 64; side of square = $\sqrt{64}$ = 8; perimeter = 4 × 8 = 32.

18. (A) Since each of five friends paid an extra ₹ 3 to cover Luxmi's portion of the bill, then Luxmi's share was 5 × ₹ 3 = ₹ 15.

Since each of the six friends had an equal share, then the total bill is 6 × ₹ 15 = ₹ 90.

19. (C) Try an example.
The difference 19992000 − 19991999 = The difference 19992001 − 19 992000, The average of 19992001 and 19991999 is 19992000. The average is always 19992000.

20. (B) My clock advances 65 minutes every 60 minutes, a ratio of 65:60, or 13:12. When my clock advances the 13 hours from 6 p.m. to 7 a.m., an accurate clock advances 12 hours, to 6 a.m.

CROSSWORD SOLUTIONS

1. Large Numbers

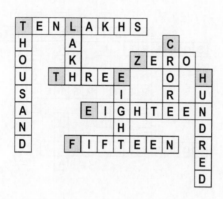

2. Factors and Multiples

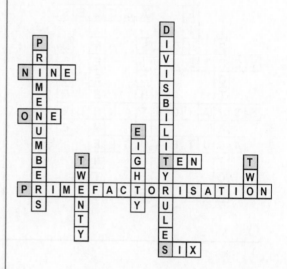

3. Fractions

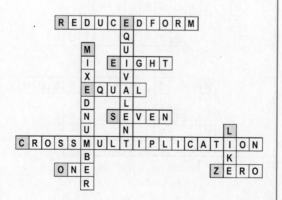

4. Decimals

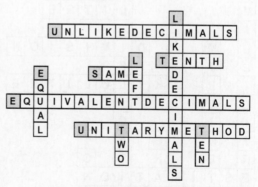

6. Geometry

```
        L       A N G L E S
        I       I
    P   N   R   N       D
V E R T E X R   E       E
    O       I   S       G
S T R A I G H T A N G L E
    A       A   M       E
    A C U T E A N G L E
    T       N   E
    O       G   N
    R A Y   L   T
            E
```

7. Mensuration

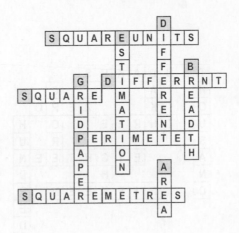

```
                    D
        S Q U A R E U N I T S
                    S   F
                    T   F   B
          G   D I F F E R R N T
    S Q U A R E   M       R E
          I       A       E A
          D       T       N D
          P E R I M E T E T H
          A       O       H
          P       N   A R A
    S Q U A R E M E T R E S
                        A
```

8. Measurement

```
      K I L O M E T R E
            U
            L   L I T R E
            T
M           I
I   M       P
L   I   D I V I S I O N
L   L   I
I   L   K I L O L I T R E
L   I   C
I   M   A
T   E   T   G       T
R   T   I   R       O
E S T I M A T I O N N E
S   R   N   A       N
    E       M       E
```

9. Data Handling

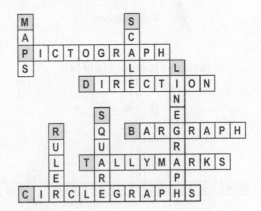

```
M               S
A               C
P I C T O G R A P H
S               L       L
          D I R E C T I O N
                        N
          S             E
    R     Q   B A R G R A P H
    U     U             R
    L   T A L L Y M A R K S
    E     R             P
C I R C L E G R A P H S
```